# THE MARCHING WOMEN

# THE MARCHING WOMEN

## INSPIRING STORIES FROM YOUNG WOMEN IN PUBLIC POLICY

MARISA LEMMA

NEW DEGREE PRESS

COPYRIGHT © 2020 MARISA LEMMA

THE MARCHING WOMEN

*Inspiring Stories from Young Women in Public Policy*

ISBN      978-1-64137-958-8   *Paperback*

          978-1-64137-779-9   *Kindle Ebook*

          978-1-64137-780-5   *Ebook*

*This book is dedicated to all trailblazing women, past, present, and future.*

# CONTENTS

———

# INTRODUCTION

———

My friend Allison Greenday was just a few months out of college when she accepted a position as a legislative aide for Delegate Dan Helmer in the Virginia House of Delegates. This was after she worked as a field organizer for Helmer's campaign and helped him win his seat in that legislature. At just twenty-two years old, Allison has already managed to make a change in her community by helping someone get into office who was not there before. And as a legislative aide, she has had even more of an opportunity to create substantial policy changes in Virginia.

I thought Allison's actions and contributions seemed unique for someone her age—after all, don't you have to be established and rich, or at a minimum age and male, to have any sort of impact on public policy?

Current statistics seem to say yes. Men still make up over three quarters of the House of Representatives—76 percent, to be exact—and three quarters of the Senate. The average age in the House is 57.6, and the average age in the Senate is a whopping 62.9.[1] So Congress, it seems, is composed of primarily old men. We see a lot of the same phenomena in state legislatures as well; in my home state of Virginia, men make up 70 percent of the state's House of Delegates and 73 percent of the state's Senate, and the average age in those bodies is 53.8 and 59.3, respectively.[2]

So how can young people, specifically young women, possibly have a voice in a political climate so dominated by older men?

I have been feeling this frustration myself recently, I'll admit. The 2016 election shattered my confidence in our electoral institutions and left me feeling voiceless in a world primarily controlled by men. My love of politics was dying at the hands of a government I felt did not represent me.

Politics wasn't always something that mattered to me. Sure, I grew up with Democratic parents who voted in every election, and when I did a mock election in fifth grade I voted for Obama. But I never really thought of myself as someone who could or should get involved in politics. I always thought one person was too insignificant to make a difference.

But my attitude changed as I got older. In fall 2015, when I was a senior in high school, I took an AP government class. At the time, the 2016 election season was just starting, so there was a lot happening in politics and so much to talk

---

1    Jennifer Manning, *Membership of the 116th Congress: A Profile*, report prepared for Members and Committees of Congress (Washington, DC: Congressional Research Service, 2020).

2    "The Virginia State Legislature," Rutgers University Center for Youth Political Participation. Updated November 18, 2019.

about. Between debates and primaries and crazy Trump tweets, there were always current events to discuss in class. This AP government class—and in particular my teacher, who is to this day one of the smartest and most passionate people I know—is really what inspired my love of politics.

The same year, I attended my first political rally. It was for Bernie Sanders, who was running against Hillary Clinton in the Democratic presidential primary. I didn't know a whole lot about Bernie, and I would never have decided on my own to go to a rally, but some friends of mine were going and asked if I wanted to tag along. We left school early so we could get in line and secure a good spot.

While we were waiting, people came over to ask if we wanted to buy buttons or make a donation. Somehow, I was persuaded to sign up for Bernie's email list even though I wouldn't turn eighteen until a month after the general election. We were there so early that we were the first people in line, so when they finally let us file in we were right up against the barrier, about five feet from the stage where Bernie would stand.

When Bernie got on stage and started to talk, I was mesmerized. I don't remember exactly what he said that night, but I do remember feeling as though he was talking directly to me. I remember feeling as though I, too, could be in politics someday. I could create change from the ground up. I had a voice and ought to use it.

So in the fall of 2016, when I got to college—fresh out of my government class, my first political rally, and the excitement of the presidential primary season, I decided this was what I wanted to study. I wanted to analyze our political institutions more in-depth and to gain a better understanding of how the system works and doesn't work. I wanted to figure out how to create positive change and how to use my voice to be part of this political movement.

I remember November 8, 2016, like it was yesterday. It was my first semester of college and I was exactly four weeks shy of being eighteen. I felt very confident that Hillary Clinton would win and become our first female president. I went to my classes that morning without a care in the world, and I came home and watched Netflix instead of doing my homework. My roommate and I couldn't wait to watch the results on the tiny little TV I had on my desk. She rolled her desk chair over to my side of the room and we turned on MSNBC, excitedly awaiting the first poll closings.

Then, the election results came in. Every time another state lit up red on the map, I felt more and more ill. By about midnight they had called the election for Trump. We didn't have it in us to stay up and wait for the last few states to tally their votes, so we turned off the TV and went to bed, feeling defeated and quite nearly in tears.

When I woke up the next morning, for a split second I forgot that Trump had won the election. I desperately hoped that I had dreamed it and that Clinton had won instead, that I was not living in the reality of an America that still hadn't elected a female president. But I was. And even worse than that, the Congress we had elected was one of the oldest in history, and there were very few women in it.

That first day after the election was a blur. My professors all looked like they were going to cry, and campus felt like it was in mourning for weeks afterward. I felt like there was no hope left to hold onto, like maybe that fire of activism that the Bernie Sanders rally had ignited in me just over a year ago was misguided. The government didn't represent me, and it wouldn't listen to me. I wasn't sure what to do. This felt like a huge step backward for America, and I didn't know what I, as a mere college student, could do to change it.

My answer came to me one windy day the following January, when I attended the Women's March on Washington. On January 21, 2017, the day after Donald Trump took his oath of office, I dragged myself out of bed at six in the morning and marched through Washington, DC, with five hundred thousand other people. I marched for hours, chanting things such as, "My body, my choice!" and "We will not go away, welcome to your first day!"

When I went to the Women's March, I felt that spark of inspiration I hadn't felt since November. I remembered people do have power; they can create change, even when circumstances seem rough. Seeing half a million people stepping up to make their voices heard was so empowering. I was part of a political movement, and it was so powerful.

I've been involved in politics quite a bit since then; I've interned in a state senator's office, seen President Obama speak, and canvassed for various political candidates. But nothing has felt as influential as the Women's March. I've never felt as seen or heard as I did that day.

That is part of why I'm writing this book. I think it's time the women of the world start making their voices heard, and it's time people start listening to them. It's time we vote to get more women in office. It's time we encourage young women in particular to get involved in politics.

It's time we continue the progress we've made.

The 2016 election was a setback, but we've come a long way since then. The number of women in Congress is at an all-time high, and the average age of Congress dropped by ten years after the 2018 midterm elections. This is due largely to the women discussed in this book and to all the other young women who, like me, have discovered the power of their voice.

Allison Greenday found her voice through campaigning. Pooja Tanjore found her voice through her involvement with Rise to Run. Alexandria Ocasio-Cortez and Cassandra Levesque found their voices through running for office. This book contains insights from these women and many more, as well as the commonalities of their success stories. These women are using their voices to put a lot of good into the world. If enough women step up and make their voices heard, we can create a real change in public policy and finally shatter the glass ceiling that's been above our heads for centuries.

So I encourage you, young women of the world, or anyone who feels like your voice is not being heard—to find your voice and get involved. It doesn't have to be something as large scale as the Women's March on Washington, but find something you're passionate about and find something you can do that makes you feel seen and heard, because it is always possible.

After all, glass ceilings were made to be broken.

# PART 1

# CHAPTER 1

# TRAILBLAZING WOMEN IN PUBLIC SERVICE AND ACTIVISM

———

*One thing I believe profoundly: We make our own history. The course of history is directed by the choices we make and our choices grow out of the ideas, the beliefs, the values, the dreams of the people.*

—ELEANOR ROOSEVELT[3]

When Hillary Clinton became the Democratic nominee for President of the United States in 2016, she made history. Never in the United States' 228-year history had a woman been the nominee of a major political party. As she stood on the stage at the Democratic National Convention accepting her nomination, she said, "Standing here as my mother's

———

3  Theresa Avila, "18 Quotes About Political Action That Will Fire You Up to Vote," Girlboss, November 2, 2018.

daughter, and my daughter's mother, I'm so happy this day has come. Happy for grandmothers and little girls and everyone in between. Happy for boys and men, too. Because when any barrier falls in America, for anyone, it clears the way for everyone."[4]

Women have been activists and public servants for at least 150 years, and they have slowly been chipping away at all the barriers in their way. Studying the historic women who have stepped up to create change in their communities is, in my opinion, a fundamental part of our understanding of current activists and public servants. We would not be where we are today without these powerful women who came before. Understanding what they went through and what they did for us is vital.

Hillary Clinton was not the first woman to knock down a barrier and clear the way for everyone else. In fact, she wasn't even the first woman to run for president. Over one hundred years earlier, in 1872, a woman named Victoria Woodhull ran for president as a member of the Equal Rights Party. She believed in women's suffrage, equal rights, and "free love," and though her campaign was unsuccessful, she paved the way for other women to run for president.[5] In 2008, she was posthumously awarded the "Ronald H. Brown Trailblazer Award," which celebrates women who were committed to

---

4    "Hillary Clinton's DNC speech: full text," CNN Politics, Updated July 29, 2016.

5    Maggie MacLean, "Victoria Woodhull," The Ohio State University Department of History, Accessed April 24, 2020.

"uplifting underrepresented groups and individuals."[6] Victoria Woodhull was truly a trailblazer for future generations of women.

One of those future daring women was Jeannette Rankin. In 1916, she became the first woman ever elected to Congress.[7] Rankin was from Montana and born in 1880, nine years before Montana became a state. When she ran for Congress, she advocated for social welfare and suffrage and won one of Montana's two seats in the House of Representatives. Her election victory came four years prior to the passage of the Nineteenth Amendment, which gave women the right to vote, so at the time she was the only woman with any federal political power. She knew this too, as she stated in her victory speech, "I am deeply conscious of the responsibility resting upon me."[8]

Rankin, in her tenure as a congresswoman, was able to set the stage for other women to have political power. While she was in Congress, she created the Committee on Woman Suffrage and opened debate on an amendment granting this. She became the only woman who has ever voted to give women the right to vote.[9]

---

6    Leonard M. Baynes, "The Celebration of the 40th Anniversary of Ronald H. Brown's Graduation from St. John's School of Law," *Journal of Civil Rights and Economic Development* 25, no. 1 (Fall 2010): 14.

7    "Milestones for Women in American Politics," Center for American Women and Politics, Rutgers University, Accessed April 24, 2020.

8    "Rankin, Jeannette," United States House of Representatives, History, Art & Archives, Accessed April 24, 2020.

9    "Jeannette Rankin: The woman who voted to give women the right to vote," National Archives, Pieces of History, January 26, 2017.

Since Rankin's historic congressional seat, women have broken down other barriers to their participation in the federal government. In 1933, Frances Perkins became the first woman ever appointed to a presidential cabinet.[10] She was Franklin Delano Roosevelt's Secretary of Labor for his entire tenure as president, and she was one of only two people who remained in the cabinet for all four terms.[11] In this role, she helped to administer several aspects of the New Deal, including the Civilian Conservation Corps and the Social Security Act, two government programs that had a huge impact on the labor force in the US[12] Since the pioneering Frances Perkins broke down this barrier eighty-six years ago, thirty-one other women have held cabinet secretary positions.[13]

It was only in more recent history that women first entered the judicial branch of the federal government. In 1981, Sandra Day O'Connor was appointed to the Supreme Court by President Ronald Reagan. She became the first woman to serve as a Supreme Court justice and the first woman with any power to shoot down laws passed by Congress. Three women currently serve on the Supreme Court: Ruth Bader Ginsburg, appointed in 1993 by President Bill Clinton; Sonia Sotomayor, appointed in 2009 by President Barack Obama; and Elena Kagan, appointed in 2010, also by President Obama. These

10   Rutgers University, "Milestones for Women."

11   Linda Alchin, "Franklin Roosevelt Presidential Cabinet," US Presidents, January 2016, Accessed April 24, 2020.

12   Jessica Breitman, "Frances Perkins," FDR Library & Museum, Accessed April 24, 2020.

13   "Women Appointed to Presidential Cabinets," Center for American Women and Politics, Rutgers University, April 12, 2019.

are the only three other women that have ever held this position.[14]

Women have made history at the state and local levels too, and these women, though less well-known than many of the national figures, are just as important. Getting involved locally can be an even better way to create change. I know from personal experience just how effective local governments can be. A couple of years ago, I worked in a state senator's office, and I saw firsthand how much easier and more effective it was to create change at a local level.

In 1887, Susanna Madora Salter became the first woman elected as mayor in the United States.[15] She was elected to serve the small town of Argonia, Kansas, which had about five hundred residents when she assumed office. Salter's story is particularly moving because she didn't even know she was on the ballot. A group of men that were against women's involvement in politics put her name on the ballot and she didn't know until the day of the election. Only after members of the Republican Party saw her name on the ballot and told her did she know what had happened. She agreed to accept the position if she won, so the Republican Party agreed to elect her to teach the men who put her name on the ballot a lesson.[16] Her win makes the story even more satisfying, since she helped pave the way for other women who had people doubting their gender's fitness for office.

---

14  Linda Lowen, "Meet the Female Supreme Court Justices," ThoughtCo, Updated October 2, 2019.

15  Rutgers University, "Milestones for Women."

16  Monroe Billington, "Susanna Madora Salter First Woman Mayor," *Kansas Historical Quarterly* 21, no. 3 (Autumn 1954): 173-183.

Shortly after that, in 1892, Laura Eisenhuth was elected super-intendent of public instruction in North Dakota, making her the first woman to ever be elected to a statewide office.[17] This was a significant advancement because in North Dakota, women could only vote on matters of education, and the superintendent race was the only one they were able to vote in. When Eisenhuth first ran for this position in 1890, she made the argument that since women could vote in this race, they could surely run in it. Unfortunately, she lost that year, and she also lost her reelection bid in 1894. But with her two-year tenure she paved the way for so many other women to run for statewide positions, both in North Dakota and in other states. In fact, when she lost in 1894, it was to another woman.[18]

At the gubernatorial level, the first strides toward equality came in 1925. This was the year Nellie Tayloe Ross of Wyoming became the first woman to be elected governor.[19] Her husband had been the governor, and after his death she was nominated and easily won the election despite not campaigning at all. As governor, she advocated for progressive policies in education and for policies that would support women and children. Ross also became the first woman to be the director of the US Mint.[20] Although she is still the only woman that has ever been governor of Wyoming, there have been

17   Rutgers University, "Milestones for Women."

18   Curt Eriksmoen, "History: ND elected first woman to be administrator of a state office," *Bismarck Tribune*, April 25, 2010.

19   Rutgers University, "Milestones for Women."

20   Tom Rea, "The Ambition of Nellie Tayloe Ross," *WyoHistory.org*, November 8, 2014.

forty-four women in thirty states that have held or currently hold gubernatorial positions.[21]

Although there have been trailblazing women in all levels of government, progress has been slow and uneven. The number of women in public service has increased, but not as quickly as we might have hoped. A woman has not yet held many important public service positions such as president. There is a huge disparity in the number of women holding these important positions. In the House of Representatives, there are currently 105 women, making up about 24 percent of the total number. Twenty-six women are in the Senate, which is 26 percent of the total number of Senators.[22]

Those statistics provide a rather grim picture of contemporary politics. It is important to mention, however, that there has been important progress made in this arena. In 2007, Democrat Nancy Pelosi became the first woman to ever be Speaker of the House.[23] She held this position until 2011 when the Republican Party regained a majority, but she took over the position again in 2019.[24] She is still the only woman to ever hold the position.

21  "History of Women Governors," Center for American Women and Politics, Rutgers University, Accessed April 24, 2020.

22  Jennifer Manning, *Membership of the 116th Congress: A Profile,* report prepared for Members and Committees of Congress (Washington, DC: Congressional Research Service, 2020).

23  Rutgers University, "Milestones for Women."

24  Sheryl Gay Stolberg, "Nancy Pelosi, Icon of Female Power, Will Reclaim Role as Speaker and Seal a Place in History," *The New York Times,* January 2, 2019.

In becoming Speaker, Pelosi has also become third in line for the presidency, which means she holds the highest position ever held by a woman.[25] This is a huge step forward. And even more recently, in the 2018 congressional elections, more women than ever before were elected. These women are younger, more diverse, and more outspoken. Freshman legislators like Alexandria Ocasio-Cortez are making headlines as part of a new and exciting influx of women in public service.

The progress we have made in terms of empowering women and breaking glass ceilings extends beyond just public service. Since the 2017 Women's March on Washington, there has been a surge in the number of women who are becoming activists and trying to create change in their communities. Since 2016, one in five Americans has attended a protest or rally, and many of those people had never attended one before.[26]

This surge in activism by women is great because more involvement from women means more informed change for those of us who feel voiceless or unrepresented by our politicians. But women have been activists since long before the Trump era. In fact, we can see evidence of activism in all the major political movements: women's suffrage, abolitionism, civil rights, and others.

Women gained the right to vote when the Nineteenth Amendment was ratified in 1920. Around the turn of the

---

25  Ibid.

26  Eric Levitz, "Trump Has Turned Millions of Americans Into Activists," *Intelligencer,* April 6, 2018.

century, and for about fifty years prior to that, there was a movement by women to try to get universal suffrage. This movement picked up quite rapidly after the 1870 passage of the Fifteenth Amendment, which extended suffrage to African American men. Many women were upset the amendment did not also include women.

One of the most prominent female activists at the time was Elizabeth Cady Stanton, who was involved in the abolitionist movement. Her frustration at the amendment's exclusion of women pushed her to also focus on the women's rights movements. She and Lucretia Mott who was another abolitionist, was inspired to go into the women's rights movement after being excluded from the World Anti-Slavery Convention in 1840—held the first women's rights convention in Seneca Falls in 1848.[27] Stanton gave speeches and wrote about the women's suffrage movement.

Another key activist, and in fact, someone who worked closely with Elizabeth Cady Stanton was Susan B. Anthony. Anthony was also an abolitionist who was frustrated women were being excluded from these efforts. Together with Stanton, she collected signatures and petitioned Congress for women's suffrage. Anthony also traveled and gave speeches, and when Stanton was unable to travel because she needed to be with her children, she would write speeches for Anthony to give.[28] The two women helped create the National American Woman Suffrage Association.

---

27  Debra Michals, "Elizabeth Cady Stanton," National Women's History Museum, 2017.

28  Ibid.

Though both Susan B. Anthony and Elizabeth Cady Stanton passed away prior to the Nineteenth Amendment's passage, their activism helped pave the way for its ratification. In fact, in 1872, Anthony tried to vote illegally and was arrested for it. After she was convicted in an extremely publicized trial, she refused to pay the fine and petitioned Congress for its remission, which forced Congress and the general public to pay attention to the issue of women's rights.[29]

A slightly lesser known but still important female activist at the turn of the twentieth century was Anna Dickinson. Like the other women of her day, her activism took the form of speaking and writing to communicate a message. Dickinson was a lecturer who gave speeches about both African American rights and women's rights; as well as other major issues of the day, and she was quite well received. She was friends with both Lucretia Mott and Susan B. Anthony, though she was not directly affiliated with the women's suffrage movement.[30] After her career as a lecturer began to falter, she used her written voice as her primary means of activism and expressed her viewpoints on issues such as interracial marriage and treatment of prisoners.

The women's suffrage movement was extremely important because it gave a voice to hundreds of thousands of people. It empowered them and it continues to empower American women. Every time I vote, I think back to the brave and persistent women who fought to get this right for me. I consider

---

29  Nancy Hayward, "Susan B. Anthony," National Women's History Museum, 2018.

30  "Anna Dickinson," National Women's History Museum, Accessed May 26, 2020.

myself infinitely lucky that I get to have a say in what my government looks like. I am eternally grateful to Elizabeth Cady Stanton, Lucretia Mott, Susan B. Anthony, Anna Dickinson, and the countless other women who helped us achieve such a huge stride forward. Without them, I would not be able to participate in my own government.

Women's activism did not stop after the passage of the Nineteenth Amendment. There was also a huge amount of activism by women in the Civil Rights Movement of the 1960s, which pushed for equal rights for African Americans. There were people we learned about in history classes, such as Rosa Parks, who famously refused to give up her seat in the front section of the bus which was the section reserved for white people—and thus, gave rise to the Montgomery bus boycott. But there were countless other women, who are perhaps less well-known, whose activism shaped the Civil Rights Movement.

Diane Nash was one of those women. After discovering the realities of segregation when she moved to Nashville for college, Nash became active in the student movement. She was the leader of the Nashville sit-ins, one of the founders of the Student Nonviolent Coordinating Committee (SNCC), and one of the leaders of the Freedom Riders, a group of activists who rode buses into the South to protest segregation.[31] She was arrested many times for her actions but refused to pay bail, stating, "We feel that if we pay these fines we would be contributing to and supporting the injustice and immoral practices that have been performed in the arrest

---

31  "Diane Nash," SNCC Digital Gateway, Accessed April 24, 2020.

and conviction of the defendants."[32] Despite these arrests and continued discrimination against African Americans throughout the US, she never gave up and continued to be an activist for positive change in her community.

But Diane Nash was far from the only female activist in the Civil Rights Movement. There were Coretta Scott King, Barbara Johns, Gwendolyn Sanders, Audrey Faye Hendricks, and countless others.

Coretta Scott King was the wife of Martin Luther King, Jr., who is perhaps the most well-known figure in the Civil Rights Movement. After he was assassinated, she carried on his work. She gave speeches and founded the King Center for Nonviolent Social Change, which sought to promote her late husband's legacy. Her activism has helped make Martin Luther King Jr. Day a national holiday and has ensured no one forgets the Civil Rights Movement.[33]

Barbara Johns was a civil rights activist who, when she was just sixteen, led a student strike at her all-black high school to protest unequal education. Her school and many of the other all-black schools did not have the resources or maintained facilities the white schools had. The court case she and other students filed was one of the cases later consolidated into *Brown v. Board of Education*, which finally did away with

---

32  "Diane Nash," Atlanta Journal-Constitution, February 1, 2017.

33  "Mrs. Coretta Scott King," About Mrs. King, The King Center, Accessed April 24, 2020.

"separate but equal" schools.[34] In fact, their case was the only one of those cases initiated by students.

Johns is a great example of a young activist who was able to make a difference in her community. Her dedication to fighting for better education for herself and her peers is quite admirable, especially since she was so young when she did this. I can't even imagine having to fight for my education at such a young age. When I was sixteen, the only thing I had to worry about was whether I would pass my driving test. I have a huge amount of respect for Barbara Johns because she had to fight for something so fundamental at such a young age.

Two other young activists in the Civil Rights Movement were Gwendolyn Sanders and Audrey Faye Hendricks, both of whom were children when they were arrested for participating in the movement.

Audrey Faye Hendricks was just nine years old when she marched in the children's march in Birmingham, Alabama, and spent a week in jail. Her parents' heavy involvement in the Civil Rights Movement spurred her participation in it.[35] Gwendolyn Sanders was a teenager when she and her sisters participated in the same march in Birmingham and were also arrested. The following day, they were attacked by fire hoses and police dogs while participating in a nonviolent protest in a park. Gwendolyn's involvement in this march and in the Civil Rights Movement more broadly helped shape the

---

34   "Barbara Johns," Americans Who Tell the Truth, Accessed May 26, 2020.

35   "Audrey Faye Hendricks," We've Got a Job, Major Players, Accessed May 26, 2020.

current racial climate in the US. When people saw the widely televised images of water hoses and police dogs attacking children, they were appalled and knew things needed to change.[36]

Even outside of these big movements, there were women who were activists in their communities. A great example of this is Gloria Steinem, who in the 1960s and 70s wrote about and organized around women's issues, becoming the spokesperson for the feminist movement. Steinem's writing is what brought her to fame nationwide and allowed her to be such a successful activist. One of her first major articles involved how the Playboy bunnies were treated, and she later went on to tackle abortion, the Equal Rights Amendment—a proposed constitutional amendment that would guarantee legal equal rights for women and thus make great strides toward full equality of the genders along with other women's issues of importance at the time.[37]

Steinem has remained a well-known figure and activist to this day. Her words have inspired other women to become activists in their communities. She and so many other women have inspired me to use my voice and stand up for what I believe in. As a writer myself, I find her words to be powerful. They inspire me to use my voice to create change as well.

As you can see, there have been so many women who have made history by being an activist in their communities, often

36  "Sisters who participated in 1963 Children's March to speak at Smithfield Library today," *AL.com*, March 10, 2016.

37  Debra Michals, "Gloria Steinem," National Women's History Museum, 2017.

closely aligned with other great social movements of the time. Today, we still see many women being activists. There are people like "Little Miss Flint," Sophie Cruz, Emma Gonzalez, Greta Thunberg, and too many others to count. These young women would not be able to be such strong activists if not for the trailblazing women that came before them. They too are setting a path for future women activists.

All of the historic women highlighted above and many others who were not mentioned but still played an active role in breaking glass ceilings and advocating for their communities—women like Hillary Clinton are able to continue breaking barriers. Clinton herself was an activist. In fact, when her husband, Bill Clinton, was President, she used her stance as First Lady to advocate for healthcare reform, trying to affect positive change in the lives of her fellow Americans. She served for many years as a public servant, as a Senator, and as President Obama's Secretary of State.[38] Her 2016 Democratic National Convention speech feels much more powerful when we know about the long line of inspiring women who came before her.

"When there are no ceilings, the sky's the limit," she told us in that speech. "So, let's keep going, until every one of the 161 million women and girls across America has the opportunity she deserves. Because even more important than the history we make tonight, is the history we will write together in the years ahead."[39]

---

38   "Hillary R. Clinton Biography," Clinton Presidential Library, Accessed May 26, 2020.

39   CNN Politics, "DNC speech."

We have come very far already, but we still have a long way to go. Hillary Clinton, the trailblazing women discussed in this chapter, and the passionate women discussed in the chapters to come provide us with the hope that all women will someday get the opportunities we deserve.

# CHAPTER 2

# WHY THERE ARE SO FEW WOMEN IN POLITICS

———

*I would much rather be the "obnoxious feminist girl" than be complicit in my own dehumanization.*

—KATHLEEN HANNA[40]

Most Americans agree there are not enough women in politics. In fact, 59 percent of people surveyed in a 2018 Pew poll believed there are not enough women in high political offices. A staggering 69 percent believed having more women in top government positions would improve the quality of life for Americans.[41] And yet, women hold less than 25 percent of seats in Congress despite making up half of America's population. So why aren't there more women in politics? What is holding women back?

---

40  Theresa Avila, "18 Quotes About Political Action That Will Fire You Up to Vote," Girlboss, November 2, 2018.

41  Juliana Menasce Horowitz, Ruth Igielnik, and Kim Parker, "Women and Leadership 2018," Pew Research Center, September 20, 2018.

For starters, women in politics experience a lot of violence and hateful rhetoric against them. There has not been a huge amount of research on this phenomenon, but the results paint a rather grim picture of politics all over the world. A study conducted in 2018 in European countries indicates more than 80 percent of women in Parliaments have experienced some sort of violence.[42] The findings of a study conducted in certain South Asian countries indicate over 60 percent of women refrain from political participation because they are afraid of violence.[43]

Many US women have also experienced this violence or threat of violence. In July 2019, a Louisiana police officer said Representative Alexandria Ocasio-Cortez is a "vile idiot" and she "needs a round."[44] Unfortunately, this is not the first time someone has threatened her with violence; in fact, she has said she regularly receives death threats. In May of that same year, someone photoshopped her into a photo with Kim Jong-Un and Fidel Castro, labeling her one of "America's adversaries." In response to this, she tweeted, "What people don't (maybe do) realize is when orgs air these hateful messages, my life changes bc of the flood of death threats they inspire. I've had mornings where I wake up & the 1st thing I do w/ my coffee is review photos of the men (it's always men) who want to kill me." It is because of threats like these, many women refrain from participating in politics.

---

42   "Violence Against Women in Politics," International Knowledge Network of Women in Politics, Accessed April 24, 2020.

43   "Violence Against Women in Politics," UN Women, 2014.

44   William Cummings, "Louisiana police officer's Facebook post says Alexandria Ocasio-Cortez 'needs a round,' report says," *USA Today,* July 23, 2019.

Representative Ilhan Omar has also recently been the recipient of violent rhetoric. In April 2019, a man in New York said he would "put a bullet" in her.[45] Around the same time, a man in Florida said he wanted to throw her off the Empire State Building.[46] In fact, she has been threatened so much she has begun bringing security with her wherever she goes. In August 2019, she shared an anonymous death threat she received that said she would "not be going back to Washington" and she would likely die at the Minnesota State Fair. With this photo, she tweeted, "I hate that we live in a world where you have to be protected from fellow humans. I hated it as a child living through war and I hate it now."

Even the president has used a lot of hateful speech about women in politics. President Trump seems to have a particular vendetta against Ocasio-Cortez, Omar, and two other Democratic congresswomen of color. He keeps telling them they should go back to where they came from and claiming they "hate our country." It's important to note all four of these women are US citizens, and all but Omar were born in the United States. Trump also tweeted a video with images of 9/11 interspersed with clips of Representative Omar speaking, which Omar said led to many new death threats against her. In a society where the president, the most powerful person in the country, will attack women who get involved in politics, it's no wonder there are so few women in Congress.

---

45  Jeff Murray and Christal Hayes, "'I'll put a bullet in her': Trump supporter charged with threatening to kill Rep. Ilhan Omar," *USA Today*, Updated April 7, 2019.

46  Christal Hayes, "Trump supporter threatens to kill Democratic lawmakers over Rep. Omar's 9/11 comments, docs say," *USA Today*, Updated April 19, 2019.

This is not just a phenomenon that we see in Washington, either; this kind of threatening language happens at the state level as well. A former member of the Minnesota House of Representatives Linda Slocum received a death threat in March 2018 after introducing a gun control bill. One night after Slocum introduced the bill, her legislative assistant answered a phone call. The man on the other end threatened to kill Slocum, and he wasn't even in her district.[47]

Another reason there are so few women in politics is because of traditional gender roles and societal standards. For a very long time, it was frowned upon for women to even enter the workforce; their job was to stay at home with the children and be traditional "homemakers." Americans' attitudes toward this has largely changed, and it is much more common and acceptable for a woman to enter the workforce instead of being a homemaker. But this antiquated mindset has a large impact on the political climate of today.

According to a 2018 Pew poll, 80 percent of Americans believe family responsibilities make it harder for women to run for office.[48] Even though it is acceptable for women to be in the workforce, they are largely expected to take care of the children and manage the household, leaving many of them with very little time to run a campaign.

These traditional gender roles do not refer solely to what women do; they also apply to the personality traits women

---

47  Tad Vezner, "Death threat allegedly called in to office of MN lawmaker who sponsored gun-control bill," *Twin Cities Pioneer Press,* March 6, 2018.

48  Pew Research Center, "Women and Leadership 2018."

are supposed to have. According to a study by the Georgetown University Center on Education and the Workforce, more than one in eight Americans believe women are too emotional to hold elected office.[49] This is a large part of why women are so underrepresented in politics; they are considered overly emotional, whether they have proven themselves to be or not, causes many people to not vote for them.

Women who show weakness are treated very differently than men who do the same thing. Former President Barack Obama has been known to tear up when addressing the nation after a major tragedy, and people have praised him for this since men who show vulnerability are largely viewed favorably. But when women do the same thing, they are considered weak and criticized for being overly emotional.

Take, for example, Hillary Clinton. She has, on multiple occasions, been called "overly emotional." Donald Trump has even called her "unstable" and "insane."[50] This is because as a woman, she is expected to keep her composure all the time. Emotional women are seen as "unfit" for political office.

As Clinton herself described it, "I'll go to these events and there will be men speaking before me, and they'll be pounding the message, and screaming about how we need to win the election, and people will love it. And I want to do the same thing. Because I care about this stuff. But I've learned that I can't be quite so passionate in my presentation. I love

49   Susan Milligan, "Women Candidates Still Tagged as Too 'Emotional' to Hold Office," *US News & World Report,* April 16, 2019.

50   Janell Ross, "Donald Trump thinks Hillary Clinton, a lady running for president, is crazy," *The Washington Post,* August 8, 2016.

to wave my arms, but apparently that's a little bit scary to people. And I can't yell too much. It comes across as 'too loud' or 'too shrill' or 'too this' or 'too that.' Which is funny, because I'm always convinced that the people in the front row are loving it."[51]

From a very young age, Clinton learned she had to control her emotions to deal with criticism from men. In a 2016 interview with Humans of New York, she told a story about taking her law school admissions test. She was one of the very few women in the room and before the test began, some men began to yell at her. They said she didn't need to be there and she would "take their spot" in law school.

"It was intense," she said. "It got very personal. But I couldn't respond. I couldn't afford to get distracted because I didn't want to mess up the test."[52] She has learned that, as a woman, she cannot get overly emotional, or she will end up facing consequences that an emotional man would not have to deal with.

Clinton often gets criticized for being too cold. For example, in a letter to the editor of The Fresno Bee, someone wrote, "Hillary Clinton was a typical, boring, over-rehearsed politician. Her bizarre talking points were delivered with no emotion, no heart and no soul."[53] She is somehow perceived

---

51 Emily Crockett, "Hillary Clinton: 'I had to learn as a young woman to control my emotions,'" *Vox*, September 8, 2016.

52 Ibid.

53 Vicki Mathiesen, "Clinton shows 'no emotion, no heart no soul,'" Letter to the editor, *Fresno Bee*, 2016.

as both too emotional and not emotional enough, a contradiction men typically don't have to face.

"I know that I can be perceived as aloof or cold or unemotional. But I had to learn as a young woman to control my emotions."[54] Hillary Clinton shows us just how tough it is to be a woman in politics and how much gender discrimination women face every day.

People have been using gender discrimination as a reason to keep women out of office for all of recent memory. In fact, according to a 2018 Pew poll, 81 percent of Americans say gender discrimination is a reason there aren't more women in politics, and about half of Americans say it is a major reason.[55]

Gender discrimination, traditional gender roles, and violence against women have all played a role in keeping many women out of politics. As a result, women are extremely underrepresented in our legislatures. But in 2018, there was a record number of women elected to Congress, which means many women are willing to go into politics despite all these barriers. Hillary Clinton, despite being criticized about how much emotion she shows, managed to climb almost all the way up the political ladder, even becoming the Democratic nominee for President of the United States. Having so many barriers to women entering the political sphere can be frustrating, but it is promising to see we are moving in the right direction and to see women continue to go into politics and fight against these obstacles.

---

54    Crockett, "Hillary Clinton."
55    Pew Research Center, "Women and Leadership 2018."

# CHAPTER 3

# WHY YOUNG WOMEN ARE IMPORTANT

———

*We do need women in civic life. We do need women to run for office, to be in political office. We need a feminist to be at the table when decisions are being made so that the right decisions will be made.*

—DOLORES HUERTA[56]

Alexandria Ocasio-Cortez took office as a representative for the state of New York in January 2019 at just twenty-nine years old. In her first year alone, she managed to shift the Democratic Party to the left and inspire so many people, all while actually getting work done. "In my first 11 months I've cosponsored 339 pieces of legislation, authored 15, took on

———

56  Theresa Avila, "18 Quotes About Political Action That Will Fire You Up to Vote," Girlboss, November 2, 2018.

Big Pharma w/ my colleagues... & exposed abuse of power," she tweeted in response to criticism from Donald Trump.[57]

I bring up Ocasio-Cortez here because, in my opinion, she truly embodies why we need young women in politics. AOC represents millennials' and women's policy priorities and effectiveness. Though she has only been in office for one term, she has affected so much change and has inspired young people everywhere, myself included, to get involved and make a difference.

As AOC herself puts it, "You can make ten years' worth of change in one term if you're not afraid."[58]

Getting young women like AOC involved in politics is extremely important because they can have a major impact on the political landscape. Women are important in politics primarily because they focus on different issues from men. Men tend to focus their efforts on terrorism and the economy, for example.[59] Women, on the other hand, focus more on education, childcare, and women's issues.

As Madeleine Albright, former US Secretary of State and current chair of the National Democratic Institute, said, "Women in government can be counted on to raise issues that others overlook, to support ideas that others oppose, and

---

57  Lauren Gambino, "'Try to keep up': how Ocasio-Cortez upended politics in her first year in office," *The Guardian*, December 24, 2019.

58  Ibid.

59  Melissa Deckman, "What Women Want: Issue Priorities for Women Voters in Election 2018," Gender Watch 2018, August 10, 2018.

to seek an end to abuses that others accept."[60] A study conducted in the 1990s showed that female legislators co-sponsored twice as many bills related to women's health as their male counterparts did.[61] Women also focus more generally on increasing quality of life. In fact, research has shown that as more women are elected, there is an increase in policy-making emphasizing quality of life.[62] Having more women in legislatures can help to shift the policy focus and create change in previously overlooked areas, making it all the more important to encourage women to run for office or to get involved in politics.

In addition to shifting the policy focus, having more women in office would shift the narrative. As Cecile Richards tells us in a 2018 Ted Talk, "Perhaps most importantly, I think all of these issues [healthcare, paid family leave, birth control, etc.] would no longer be seen as 'women's issues.' They would just be seen as basic issues of fairness and equality that everybody can get behind."[63]

Aside from focusing on different issues than men, women provide other valuable assets to politics and public policy. Another benefit women can bring to politics is their effectiveness as legislators. Women are, in general, more effective

---

60  Madeleine Albright, "A hidden reality: Violence against women in politics," *CNN*, March 8, 2016.

61  Sarah Kliff, "The research is clear: electing more women changes how government works," *Vox*, March 8, 2017.

62  Sandra Pepera, "Why Women in Politics?" Women Deliver, February 28, 2018.

63  Cecile Richards, "The political progress women have made—and what's next," filmed November 2018 at TEDWomen 2018, Video, 16:56.

as legislators and can get twice as many of their bills passed in one session of Congress than men can. Women also have a higher likelihood of trying to reach across the political aisle and are better at responding to constituents' concerns and getting money allocated to their districts.[64] This high effectiveness is due to a multitude of factors, including the fact that women tend to be overqualified to run for office. This is because women tend to underestimate their qualifications for a position and thus only run for office when they are overqualified, but I digress.

Cecile Richards really summed it up when she said, "All the evidence is that when women actually have the chance to serve, they make a huge difference and they get the job done."[65]

It's not just women who are important in the political landscape. Young people can also bring a fresh new perspective to politics. For starters, they are larger generations. Millennials—typically defined as those born in the 80s and 90s—and Generation Z—typically defined as those born in the 2000s or later—are much larger than previous generations, especially Generation X. This means more voices need to be represented. As of 2020, millennials make up 25 percent of the population and Generation Z makes up 26 percent. Baby boomers and Generation X make up 21 percent and 20 percent, respectively.[66] This means we need more people

---

64   Deckman, "What Women Want."

65   Richards, "Political progress."

66   "US Population by Age and Generation in 2020," Knoema, Updated April 16, 2020.

getting involved in public policy, specifically young people; they need to represent all these additional voices to make sure everyone can be heard.

But the proportion of millennial and Generation Z representatives in our legislatures is minuscule, even taking into account the fact that Generation Z is not old enough to be in Congress. No millennials are in the Senate and only twenty-seven in the House, making up less than 1 percent of the legislature.[67] We need more young people to represent us in our legislature to speak on behalf of the younger generations.

Another benefit of having young people involved in politics is they understand technology, which makes it much easier to spread a message and keep in touch with constituents. It also makes it easier to deal with issues of privacy; for example, in a Senate hearing about privacy policy, older Senators asked questions to Mark Zuckerberg the younger generation did not need to ask. "The questions that he was getting asked about security and privacy were asinine," said Greg Davis, a millennial who watched the hearing. "We need leadership that actually understands tech."[68]

But beyond that, young people also focus on the issues. In a Hamilton College poll, 95 percent of respondents said candidates' positions on the issues were very important to them when deciding who to vote for. This was a far greater

67  "The 116th United States Congress," Rutgers University Center for Youth Political Participation. Updated April 18, 2019.

68  Laurie Kellman and Hannah Fingerhut, "Young people are looking for younger leaders, poll finds," PBS News Hour, July 30, 2018.

percentage of people than those who said candidates' appearance or race was very important.[69]

Young people want politicians to address their concerns, specifically those that matter directly to them. Electing young politicians is the best way for them to do that. After all, who better to represent young people than young people? Younger people will have many of the same generational experiences, so they will know more about what is important to this generation of individuals.

For example, many generations of people experienced 9/11, but young people experienced it in a very different light than older generations. Millennials were either still children or had just become adults when 9/11 happened, so many of us don't remember this tragedy. I know I personally don't remember 9/11 or life before 9/11, so strict airport security and a focus on counterterrorism seem to have been present my whole life. Older generations, however, do remember life before 9/11, so terrorism feels like a much more present threat.

As another example of this generation gap: Many people have seen the rise in prominence of social issues like women's and LGBTQ rights, but young people view them in a much different context than older generations. The world millennials and Generation Z are growing up in is much more accepting of rights for women and members of the LGBTQ community, and these generations have a more progressive view of gender and sexuality. The more young people we see in politics, the

69   "Political Attitudes of Young Americans," Hamilton College, Accessed May 26, 2020.

better it will be for these younger generations. They can be the voice for their generation and make sure the issues they care about are represented in politics.

The biggest reason, perhaps, that young people are important in politics is they are not stuck in their ways. Older people tend to get caught up in the way things have always been and are much more resistant to change than their younger counterparts. Young people are unafraid to break away from the status quo. To use an example from above, young people are much more accepting of same-sex marriage than older people. 73 percent of people ages eighteen to twenty-nine were in favor of it, as opposed to just 38 percent of those sixty-five and older.[70]

It is very easy for older generations to see problems and just accept this is the way things have always been done, but younger generations are less content to let these problems persist. They are motivated to go out and change things rather than just accept things as they are. Young people like to protest. In fact, according to data from Orb, people younger than forty are up to 17 percent more likely to prefer informal political participation, such as protesting, than people older than forty.[71] This is quite significant because it means young people are more likely to go out and protest when they see a problem in our society, whereas the older generations are less inclined to do so.

70   Hannah Fingerhut, "Support steady for same-sex marriage and acceptance of homosexuality," Pew Research Center, May 12, 2016.

71   Dan Morrison and Chris Tyree, "Generation Activist," Orb, Accessed May 26, 2020.

I have definitely found this to be true. As a young person myself, I have seen how politically active people my age are through well-attended protests and marches at my school. I have also participated in quite a few marches and signed quite a few petitions during my lifetime, and these have both been really powerful means for change. All of the young people I've met are passionate about improving people's lives and are not content to just leave things "the way they've always been."

As we can see, women and young people both play a vital role in politics and public policy. They can shift the focus of the legislature and provide a voice for underrepresented populations. When young women get involved in public policy, we have the potential for even more powerful change, so it is extremely important to get young women involved in the political arena. The following chapters will provide a guide for how to do this and how to create meaningful change in our communities.

# PART 2

# CHAPTER 4

# FIND YOUR PASSION

———

*Passion is energy. Feel the power that comes from focusing on what excites you.*

—OPRAH WINFREY[72]

Passion, for me, is strongly linked to frustration and anger. I find myself frustrated and angry about politics quite often, every time there is a terrible tragedy and we still don't have legislation to prevent another one; every time the president says or does something horribly racist, sexist, xenophobic, or homophobic and people still somehow support him; every time Congress fails to pass important legislation due to partisan bickering; and so many other infuriating incidents.

Sometimes I wonder why I want to pursue a career in public policy. It's easy to feel like nothing is ever going to get better because the same things keep happening over and over again. But it is precisely because of these frustrating

---

72  Dave Kerpen, "15 Inspiring Quotes on Passion (Get Back to What You Love)," Inc.com, March 27, 2014.

and disheartening events that I want to go into public policy. They give me the passion to create change so tragedies stop happening and so people in our government stop getting away with discrimination and partisan bickering. I am passionate about creating change because I know we can do better than this.

Passion, it turns out, is extremely important.

In 2019, Savannah Rogers graduated from Washington State University with a double major in strategic communications and political science. During her senior year, she was the president of the Associated Students of Washington State University (ASWSU), the university's student government. She joined ASWSU her freshman year, primarily because she wanted to make friends—and because there was free pizza at the meetings—but why she joined isn't really important.

"I really loved the work that we were doing," said Savannah. "I loved having a voice at the university level and getting to help make those big changes that do impact students."

Through student government, Savannah was able to make important change at her school, including raising money for an endowment meant to fund mental health and sexual violence prevention on campus. Getting involved in politics, even at the most local level, helped her affect change, all of which stemmed from her passion to aid and support others in her community. Student government helped Savannah discover her enthusiasm for politics and now she is working for a congressperson, making even more of a difference in her community.

I have found, by talking to people like Savannah, that having a passion for something is one of the most effective ways to create change. When you are passionate about something, it is so much easier to put in the work needed to affect change in that area. Our passions, be them a certain policy area, campaign work, or something else entirely, are what push us into politics, and what inspire us to be the change we wish to see in our communities.

Passion can be defined in many different ways. Leo Babauta, writer of the blog "Zen Habits," describes passion as "the thing that will get you motivated to get out of bed in the morning, to cry out, 'I'm alive! I'm feeling this, baby!'" Oliver Emberton says passion is "an emotion specifically intended to make you go crazy and work...at something because your brain believes it could rock your world."[73] In other words, your passions are the things that inspire you to go out and work hard at an endeavor.

America as a whole has become more passionate about political issues over recent years. Since 2016, one in five Americans have attended a protest or rally.[74] Since 2017, there have been over seventeen thousand protests with over eleven million attendees.[75] Americans are extremely passionate about change and about making their voices heard. This is a relatively recent change, largely sparked by outrage over President Trump's election.

---

73   Lidiya K, "How 15 Successful People Describe Passion," Let's Reach Success, January 24, 2020.

74   Eric Levitz, "Trump Has Turned Millions of Americans Into Activists," *Intelligencer,* April 6, 2018.

75   "Statistics," Count Love, Updated May 26, 2020.

I myself am passionate about democracy and social issues and ensuring everyone has a voice in our political arena. I find myself inspired by those who have pointed out the numerous injustices in our system and proposed ways to fix them. I especially find myself inspired by empowered women—the Ruth Bader Ginsburgs and the Hillary Clintons of the world—who have stood up and made their voices heard in our society. But, as author Mark Manson points out, "Doing what you love is not always loving what you do."[76] Politics can be quite frustrating at times and I often find myself feeling defeated or voiceless. I don't always love politics—especially given how combative and volatile the political climate has become, but it is still my passion. and I will continue to do what I love.

Sometimes our known passions can help us discover other passions. Take, for example, my friend Allison Greenday. Her interest in politics started in high school when she read a book called *Little Princes* by Conor Grennan. It was about human trafficking, and it really got her interested in human rights. When she started college at William & Mary, she chose public policy as a backup major, but ended up "getting really interested in all of the nuances." Being a public policy major helped her further realize her enthusiasm for politics. She completed an honors thesis her senior year in which she studied food insecurity in local areas and how you can address complex problems at the local level. She discovered with this honors thesis that "a local government is really uniquely situated to help their own people in ways that might be overlooked at a higher level for efficiency reasons."

---

76   Lidiya K, "Describe Passion."

It was this discovery that pushed her into local politics. After graduating from William & Mary in May 2019, Allison was hired as a field organizer for Democrat Dan Helmer's campaign for the state of Virginia's House of Delegates. Virginia has a bicameral legislature, with a Senate and a House of Delegates, and does its elections in odd-numbered years, unlike the federal House and Senate.

"Field organizing is," Allison describes, "basically the boots-on-the-ground work." Her job included knocking on doors, making phone calls, and talking to voters. She spent months talking directly to voters, finding out what mattered to them, reminding them where their polling place is, and trying to persuade them to vote for Helmer. She talked to almost every voter in the district—and talked to some of them more than once—to get a sense of where Helmer's voters were and how to reach them. When she wasn't canvassing, she was calling people in search of volunteers. She called people in the area who had volunteered in the past or anyone who had expressed interest in volunteering for Helmer. She would even cold call people looking for volunteers.

"The goal is to get people involved," said Allison. "A lot of people want to be involved in their local political arena and they just don't know how. And so, you know, we get people who'd be like, 'Well yeah, okay, I can come knock some doors. I can come make some phone calls.' And it was a really great way to get people engaged in their own community."

While many of Allison's days as a field organizer were hectic and stressful, nothing really compared to Election Day. In her words, Election Day was "everything you would want to watch a movie of"—stressful, with lots of intense emotions, and ultimately culminating in a huge success.

On Election Day, Allison woke up in the house of one of Helmer's supporters, someone who had agreed to let the field organizers crash at their house for a couple days. "You kind of wake up in this weird calm," she told me. "We all woke up and we're like. 'Okay, let's do it'." She was given four packets of doors to knock on—meaning she was assigned about two hundred houses—and was told to make sure people knew their voting locations and what time they were going to go vote. She pulled a muscle in her foot in the morning, but since this was the most important day of the entire campaign, she had no choice but to press on despite the pain.

Everyone on Helmer's staff was feeling the pressure because this was expected to be a close race—in fact, in the prior election cycle, there had been a recount, and the winner had won by just ninety-nine votes. "Oh my god...I'm not doing this right. We're going to lose this election by like three votes and it's going to be my fault," Allison said of the pressure. "And I found out later that all of us apparently had that running through our heads."

As the day went on, she was keeping an eye on reported turnout in the precincts. Virginia does its statewide elections on odd years—or "off-years," as they are sometimes known—and since 2019 was just legislature elections and not a gubernatorial election, this was the "off-off" year. But despite being the "off-off" year, lots of voters went to the polls. "By ten a.m., it was 8 percent turnout, which is crazy high," Allison said. In the 2015 elections, the last "off-off" year election, turnout for this district had been 29.3 percent for the entire day, so the fact that they had reached 8 percent that early in the day was huge.[77]

As Allison and the other members of Helmer's staff watched the reports on turnout coming in, they went back and forth between "Oh my god, we're going to do it" and "Oh no, this is going to be terrible." But by 7 p.m., when all the polls closed, they had to accept the fate of the race was now out of their hands.

Helmer had arranged an election night watch party at a local bar, which is where Allison headed after the polls closed. She walked into the party and made the rounds, talking to all the volunteers. "And then the next thing I know, I turned around and there's this little corner where every single staff member that's at the party is huddled," she described. "Everybody has a different website on their phone—like New York Times, Washington Post, VPAP [the Virginia Public Access Project, a nonpartisan group whose mission is to inform voters]—and they're just like, 'We're obsessively watching returns all night'."

They huddled together all night, watching as the various precincts tallied and reported results. Many of the primarily Republican precincts reported first, but then the more Democratic precincts began to report and they became more and more optimistic about the outcome of the race.

---

77  "General Assembly Turnout Varied in 2015," Virginia Public Access Project, August 26, 2019.

"Thirty minutes later, as we were, like, kind of all hugging each other and ready for somebody to call it, you just hear some random person in the middle of this crowd just shout out, 'New York Times just called it for Helmer,' and the entire room just exploded."

Allison says it's impossible to describe exactly how she felt in that moment, but there was no greater feeling. She had been working eleven-hour days for the last five months and according to her, "There's something really just…gut rewarding to know that… all of that has paid off."

So what's next for Allison? Believe it or not, working on a campaign did not diminish her love for politics. In fact, it gave her an even greater appreciation and passion for politics. Helmer offered her a job as a legislative aide in his office during the legislative session, which lasts from early January through late February.

"I think it's an exciting time to be a woman in politics because you're really seeing that kind of surge," said Allison. "And it's fun to be part of it and fun to stand up and be like, 'Yeah, I'm here too.'" Allison's actions and her work as a field organizer had real and meaningful consequences. It's so inspiring to see that kind of change coming from an ordinary woman who followed her passions wherever they led.

Like Allison, I first developed an enthusiasm for politics while I was in high school. I remember doing debates in my AP government class and not being able to understand why some people didn't have the same beliefs as me on things like abortion and gun control and healthcare. As I started to pay attention to the news, I realized many members of the government and many of the people running for president didn't have the same beliefs as me either. *Isn't the whole idea of a democracy that the government is supposed to represent the people?* I thought. I couldn't just sit back and let the government continue to create laws and policies I didn't agree with. I needed to get involved myself, to make sure my elected officials heard my voice and democracy still functioned the way it ought to.

This passion for democracy and making my voice heard is what has inspired me to go to rallies and marches. This has continued to carry me. Every time I feel frustrated and wonder why I even bother studying government, this pursuit of equal representation is what I return to.

## FIND YOUR COMMUNITY

For some people, passion starts at a very young age. Maya Hossain is a third-year political science major at Amherst College and has what she calls a "burgeoning political career." But she has been involved in politics since way before she started college. "I would say my involvement with politics has far preceded any of my academic pursuits of it," she told me.

Her father was instrumental in mobilizing the Northern Virginia Muslim American community, especially after 9/11, when anti-Muslim sentiment skyrocketed. He helped get people engaged in politics and get Muslim Americans to run for office and represent their community. The example her father set was what really laid the foundation for Maya's interest in politics. "He served, like, as a template for me, of what I cared about and how I was passionate about under-represented minorities in politics."

"When I got to university, I started engaging with politics on a more academic level and studying Muslim Americans as more of an intellectual political unit," Maya stated. She began to explore the various areas within political science and developed a more academic understanding of how the political system works, specifically how it works for the community she has always cared very deeply about. She recently began a senior thesis project which will focus on post 9/11 Muslim American women and how they have very quickly moved up through the political ranks. According to a Pew study, in 2018 there were about 3.45 million Muslims in the United States, making up about 1.1 percent of the population.[78] However, only about three hundred Muslims are holding a political office as of 2018.[79] This means that Muslims are drastically underrepresented in politics, although more of them have been getting involved in politics in recent years.

In summer 2019, in between her sophomore and junior years of college, Maya was an intern in Representative Jennifer Wexton's office. During this internship, Maya did research on religious organizations within Representative Wexton's district and how they could reach these groups of people to create a stronger connection between them and their representatives. Engaging with underrepresented minorities

---

78 Besheer Mohamed, "New estimates show US Muslim population continues to grow," Pew Research Center, January 3, 2018.

79 Samantha Raphelson, "Muslim Americans Running for Office In Highest Numbers Since 2001," *NPR*, July 18, 2018.

and specifically Muslim Americans, has always been high on Maya's list of priorities. So, despite exploring other interests—such as immigration reform—while participating in this internship, she also found a way to devote her energies to engaging with this community.

Maya's post-grad plans are still up in the air. But regardless of what she decides to do after college, she is certain she will continue advocating for Muslim Americans. "I care so thoroughly about Muslim engagement in politics that anything that I can find that keeps young Muslim people, especially young Muslim women, visible and actively engaged in either running for office or engaged with their legislators, I think something in that vein will be in my future." Maya has explored a lot of different areas of policy, both domestic and international, and has involved herself in the political scene in many different ways, but ultimately the thing she keeps going back to is advocacy for underrepresented minorities, specifically Muslims.

Another young woman who has found a passion for her community is Anika Manzoor. Anika is the executive director and a co-founder of the Youth Activism Project, which provides teens with the resources and skills needed to become activist leaders. Her passion for youth engagement started when she was twelve after she was invited to a session about gender disparity in education in developing countries. The woman leading the session asked them a question that changed Anika's life: "Do you want to be architects of a movement to address this injustice?"

"It was the first time I could remember an adult treating me as an equal," she said of that moment. "It was empowering. So, I said yes, and that day, my friends and I founded the very first campaign of the Youth Activism Project." The campaign was called School Girls Unite, and it focused on fundraising and policy advocacy.

"Being part of this level of change-making before I could even vote was transformative," she said. The agency she felt through her work with School Girls Unite was empowering and after speaking to other girls who went through this program, she realized a lot of them felt the same way. Youth activism, she realized, was so important to policy and to the future.

"We need to make youth activism a global norm. We need to spark more youth activists globally to set them on the path for lifelong advocacy." Because of this sentiment and her passion for this issue, she works for the Youth Activism Project. She believes deeply that youth engagement and activism are important. Anika fights for her community and uses her passion to create positive change in the lives of young people everywhere.

## HOW TO FIND YOUR PASSION

Diana Raab provides tips for those of us who may not know what our passions are. To find your life passion, she says, you should think about when you feel happiest, what you love talking about, what you've always dreamed of doing, and what your values are, among other things.[80] These are the ways to figure out what it is you should be devoting your energy to and what it is you're most passionate about. Different people have different political passions, and so do different generations. According to YPulse, millennials and Generation Z are particularly passionate about abortion and birth control, violence against women, animal welfare, bullying, and gender equality.[81] These are rather different than the issues important to Generation X. The discrepancy between important issues in these generations represent a shift in the cultural climate.

Maya Hossain's secret to finding your passion is simple. "Find a community that you care about, and link the causes you care about to the community because, you know, all this politics and public policy means nothing if we can't, you know, find people that we care about in it," she said. Maya's story shows us passion can get you a long way. Find what you're passionate about—be it a group of people, a cause, or both—and let that drive your political participation. Regardless of the other political involvement you might have, always come back to that group of people or that cause and fight for it.

**HOW DO I USE THIS PASSION?**

Maya, Anika, and Allison are fine examples of people finding and using their passion, but for many of us, figuring out

---

80  Diana Raab, "What's Your Passion?" Psychology Today, June 12, 2017.

81  "The 15 Issues Gen Z & Millennials Are Most Passionate About," YPulse, February 26, 2018.

how to do that is hard. I know I personally have struggled with identifying and acting on my political passions. Before I discovered I like to write, I found myself overwhelmed and unsure of how best to make my voice heard in politics. I knew what I cared about but didn't know how to translate that enthusiasm into something tangible.

Luckily, there are organizations that can help with that. One of these organizations is Rise to Run, a non-profit that focuses on getting progressive young women involved in politics. Rise to Run partners with local organizations to help identify opportunities for young women to improve their communities and trains them to run for office.

Pooja Tanjore is the former Virginia State Director of Rise to Run. One of the coolest parts of her job was getting to match girls up with internships they'd like. When trying to find something for them, the main question Pooja asked was, "What do you want from this experience?" She asked them if they had particular people or organizations they really care about and tried to find an internship that would be a good fit for them.

"Having a passion, I think, is...a huge, huge deal," she says. "And having a passion and being able to be vocal about it gets you from being a girl that goes to TJ [a science and technology magnet school in Northern Virginia] that builds satellites with NASA to someone who's now, like, a poli sci major in college. It moves you. Just tell me what you love and we'll find a place. There's a place for everyone." Rise to Run was great because it took the passions people already had and showed them how to use that enthusiasm to do good in their communities.

Rise to Run was especially great for Pooja because it allowed her to use her passions to help other people find theirs. She has always known helping people is something she is passionate about, especially given her family's history of child marriage. Pooja's great-grandmother was in her teens when she got married, and it had a huge impact on her life. It prevented her from getting an education because she got pregnant soon afterward. Her husband died when their two kids were very young, which meant she had to raise her children on her own. They lived in poverty and it was very difficult for her children to get an education, though her daughter, Pooja's grandmother, did go on to become a doctor in spite of it all, after eventually securing funding.

Her grandmother's and great-grandmother's struggles are what pushed Pooja into politics. She was left wondering if things might have been different had there been more women in the government during her relatives' lifetimes. If there were more women, maybe someone would have tried to help her great-grandmother and things would have been easier for her family. Through Rise to Run, Pooja got to take this passion for helping people and use it to encourage other young women to go into government and make other people's lives easier.

Rise to Run unfortunately disbanded in Virginia earlier this year due to funding obstacles, but there are a plethora of other organizations that help women get into politics, including the National Organization for Women, the League of

Women Voters, and Emily's List—all of which help people find and use their passions for change.

Passion can come from many different places. It can push us in many different directions. Allison is fond of human rights and local government, Maya is interested in helping Muslim-Americans, Pooja is passionate about getting women in politics, and I'm interested in helping everyone find their voice. We all have different stories and different backgrounds, but we are brought together by our passion for change, and that passion is the most powerful tool we have. So, I encourage all of you to find your passion. Find whatever it is that inspires you and use that to make a difference in your community.

# CHAPTER 5

# BE ACTIVE NOW AND START LOCAL

———

*This is a time for bold measures. This is the country, and you are the generation.*

—BONO[82]

Pooja Tanjore gave her first official speech at a Loudoun County Democrats meeting when she was just sixteen. She asked if she could come give a speech at this meeting, expecting there to be only a few people there. She had no idea when she asked that this would be one of the biggest meetings of the year for the Loudoun County Democrats. But she got up on stage and gave her speech anyway. For the first time ever, she told her family's story and asked for help from the room. After this speech, she had congressmen and state senators come up to her and hand her their cards, which she said was quite surreal.

———

82 Adam Fletcher, "Quotes about Youth + Social Change," Freechild Institute, January 28, 2020.

Rise to Run, the organization Pooja worked for, focused primarily on high school-aged girls because it's easiest to encourage political involvement when people are about fifteen or sixteen. As Pooja puts it, "That is when you are the most excited and empowered and ready to mobilize." Pooja was just fifteen when she first got involved; she didn't even have a high school diploma at the time, let alone an advanced level of education. Organizations like Rise to Run made it so easy for young women like her to get involved in their communities.

Getting involved in politics at a young age is critical. Early involvement leads to continued involvement, which is how real change happens. When you're young, it can seem hard to get a foot in the door, but there are tons of ways to get involved locally and begin to affect change early on.

I know firsthand how getting involved locally helps people get involved early on. I had always imagined myself working for the federal government and scoffed at the idea of working in a state or local government office. But despite this mindset, when the opportunity presented itself, I took an internship in a state senator's office my sophomore year of college. It was through this internship I realized the true effect of local governments and I saw how much the senator I was working for cared about his district and how much he tried to improve it. Getting involved in local government and seeing firsthand just how much of an effect it can have certainly increased my passion for politics and my desire to stay involved.

While I didn't get involved until college, for many people, high school is the best time to enter the world of politics.

Maya Hossain is a perfect example of this. Maya began officially getting involved in politics the summer before her freshman year of high school when she worked on her first campaign. Since she was only thirteen years old, she was doing very basic work such as phone banking and canvassing. However, the campaign was very understaffed at the beginning, so, despite being so young, she ended up with greater responsibilities, including recruiting and training volunteers. Maya continued working on campaigns all throughout high school and gained practical political experience, but she switched gears a little bit after she got to Amherst and began to study politics on a more academic level.

Even though her political work in high school was focused largely on domestic politics—specifically advocacy for underrepresented minorities—Maya's academic work has focused primarily on international politics. "I, often, at school, will center my research internationally since so much of my actual work is related to domestic affairs." She worked as a research assistant for one of Amherst's political science professors and, in this role, she studied the social media usage of African leaders, specifically presidents. Her research project was trying to figure out whether African leaders were using social media platforms, specifically Twitter, to communicate with their constituents as extensively as political leaders in the US, Canada, or the UK.

Maya has, through some of her political science classes, been able to combine her interest and experience in domestic politics with her slowly growing knowledge of international politics. Her favorite class at Amherst was "Gender and Right-Wing Populism," which looked at populist movements in the

US, in India, and throughout Europe—and also international movements such as the radical Islamist movements—and the role gender played in all of them.

The summer between her sophomore and junior years of college, Maya was an intern in the office of Representative Jennifer Wexton, who represents a district in Northern Virginia. One of the main things she did in this role was write a policy memo to send to Representative Wexton's legislative aide. She and the other interns were given a lot of freedom over what to include in that memo, so Maya chose to write about an immigration reform she was really passionate about. It focused specifically on lowering green card and citizenship application fees because they were "astronomically high," according to Maya.

At the time, becoming a citizen cost $640 and obtaining a green card cost $1,760.[83] These outrageous fees—not to mention the two thousand dollars in fees, at least, for a lawyer—are a huge barrier to obtaining the privileges of citizenship. "Since the Northern Virginia community is so full of incoming immigrants and it's got a lot of movement of immigrants, I thought it would be really relevant to have that brought to the attention of the Representative," Maya said about the immigration memo.

So what's next for Maya? She's honestly not sure. "After working for Congresswoman Wexton, I found myself wanting access to politics from a different angle," she said. "I don't

---

83  Annalisa Merelli, "Trump is trying to make it too expensive for poor American immigrants to stay," *Quartz*, December 6, 2019.

know if legislative work is exactly the angle I want to go in, but I'm definitely open to it someday in the future." Like most political science students, she has considered law school, and in fact is likely to go in that direction, claiming, "The reason I feel so hesitantly about jumping right back into legislative work is because I was writing things like policy memos and doing that kind of heavy hands-on research. I found that, no matter how much research I do about the issue, there's only so much I can do without really understanding what laws look like and how they look when they're actually being applied."

Maya's story shows us that early involvement in politics can really spark a chain reaction. She got involved in high school and has remained involved throughout her college career in different capacities. She was just thirteen when she first began her work in politics, but she was able to have a real impact on her community, especially by starting locally and working her way up to the federal level. Maya has no intention of stopping her political momentum and wants to continue this involvement she began all those years ago.

## YOU'RE NEVER TOO YOUNG TO GET INVOLVED

Lucy Greenman was a sophomore in high school when her local federal representative, Barbara Comstock, paid a visit to her chemistry lab. Lucy attended the Loudoun Academy of Science, a magnet school where students attend their science and math classes while going to their local high school for all of their other classes. Comstock came into Lucy's chemistry class and asked her to explain the lab they were doing.

She didn't have a background in science, so even though Lucy tried to explain the lab, she felt like the representative wasn't really understanding it. After the visit, Comstock used a picture of Lucy on her Facebook page, a picture Lucy didn't even know was taken.

Science is extremely important to Lucy. She went to a specialized science high school and has studied, in depth, a lot of scientific issues, specifically those related to public health. Earlier in her high school career, she had lobbied in DC about embryonic stem cell research, an issue on which she has significantly more knowledge than the average congressperson. That same representative who visited her chemistry lab had voted against funding the scientific research Lucy had lobbied about.[84]

The combination of these experiences is what pushed Lucy into her first campaign job. She was frustrated that her representative would post a photo from her science class when this same representative had been so opposed to the science presented to her in DC.

"I was upset that she was using me and my high school to represent something that I didn't think she really stood for," said Lucy. That's why, when she received a flyer saying Comstock had voted for a bill that required women in their first trimester to have a transvaginal ultrasound before being allowed to have an abortion—something Lucy fundamentally disagreed

---

84    Rachel Weiner, "Outside groups launch attacks in Va. congressional race," *The Washington Post,* October 14, 2014.

with—she became more and more determined to oust her in favor of someone who did believe in science.

At the time, though, Lucy was not yet eighteen, so she was not old enough to vote.

"I couldn't vote her out so I had to go into the campaign," she said, and that's exactly what she did. In the fall of Lucy's senior year of high school, September 2017, she began working for Jennifer Wexton, who was mounting a campaign against the incumbent Comstock. Lucy was a finance intern, which meant her job included research on potential donors and how much they could be expected to contribute. Doing this research would make it easier for the campaign to reach out and make reasonable donation requests. Later in the campaign, Lucy also had to do phone banking and canvassing.

Thanks to Lucy and the others who worked on the campaign, Wexton won the race and overthrew the two-term incumbent. By this point, November 2018, Lucy was in her first semester of college, so she wasn't at the election night watch party with the others on Wexton's staff. In fact, she was at a required event for her Spanish class when the race was called. "I wasn't even watching the results yet. I was in a Spanish house activity watching a movie…And I came out of the movie to like thirty texts and missed calls from my boss and my family and random people from home."

Lucy hopes someday to be able to combine her two biggest interests, science and politics. She would like to figure out a way to make scientific information accessible to the public as there is currently a lot of misinformation being spread about science. "I think that the public generally has a poor understanding of science, and especially with sensationalized headlines and that sort of thing that are trying to attract readers and not necessarily educate them. We end up with a lot of public distrust in science. And then it's not well reflected in policy because legislators don't necessarily understand it either." She doesn't know of a position yet that will allow her to do this, but now that she has experience in both politics and science, she has a good foundation upon which to build.

And campaigns, she believes, were a good place to start for her. After Wexton's campaign, she worked on a campaign for Suhas Subramanyam, who was running for delegate in the Virginia House of Delegates. "In my experience campaigns are super, super friendly to young people who want to get engaged. Actually, on Suhas's campaign, Suhas was probably the oldest person on the staff at thirty-two. Our campaign manager was twenty-three, our field organizer was nineteen, and the rest of us were, like, college freshmen. So yeah, it's super easy to get your feet wet and then quickly get into these leadership positions if you have the energy to do it."

"I think after 2016 especially, there's a ton of infrastructure for getting involved as a complete beginner," she said. So, although campaigns are a good place to start, they are not necessarily the only way to follow in her footsteps. "If you're particularly interested in one issue, there is probably an organization for it." Lucy's big issue is science, and through working on Representative Wexton's campaign, she found a way to make her voice heard on that one issue. Part of the reason for her success is that she started locally to affect change in her hometown. Both of the candidates she worked for won their respective races, so there is actual proof that getting involved locally is possible and beneficial. Lucy provides an inspiring story for all young women because she went out and made a change in the issues she cared about, even when she was too young to vote.

## COLLEGE CLUBS CAN BE EFFECTIVE WAYS TO CREATE CHANGE

I imagine, after reading this, it's easy to feel discouraged and think if you didn't get involved in politics in high school, there's no point. But that is definitely not true. In fact, I myself didn't really get involved in politics until college. I had been to a political rally in high school, but I had never worked on a campaign or in any legislative offices. I didn't even canvass for the first time until I was a sophomore in college. But despite not getting involved until college, I have still been able to make a difference in my community and have continued to stay involved. It's never really too late to get involved in local politics.

An excellent example of this is Camryn Cobb. Camryn is a consumer journalism student at the University of Georgia and a future author, but her real passion lies with politics. In fact, she has always been interested in politics. "I think I always wanted to work for the government, just because my dad's military," she said. "And it was kind of always an avenue that I knew." In high school, she would watch Scandal, a show about politics, and read books about politics to learn more about it, but for a long time she just considered it a hobby. She never envisioned a career in politics.

But by her second year of college, she had changed her mind. Now, she has her sights set on going into politics; in fact, she wants to be a US Senator someday.

What caused Camryn's change of heart? The story starts her freshman year of college, when she joined the Young Democrats club on her campus. She was involved in other extracurriculars, so she was never super active in the organization, but it still managed to have a huge influence on her life. She still remembers the very first meeting she ever went to. The county commissioner was there to talk about gentrification.

The University of Georgia is located in Athens, which is the poorest city in the state. The university generates a lot of money, but outside of that, the city is really poor. There has been a lot of gentrification in the area and as a result, people who live there are being pushed out of Athens. According to Camryn, most of the students at the university are unaware of this problem, even though this is happening in the town they all live in.

At this Young Democrats meeting, Camryn spoke to the county commissioner, who happened to be a PhD student at the university, and another PhD student. She began helping them on a gentrification project they were working on.

"When I got on board, they were in the process of mapping out and going to every door in a particular historic black community called the Reece-Hancock Corridor," she told me. They were collecting data on who the residents were and how they were being affected by gentrification. Camryn's job was to do oral history interviews and to collect information on the housing locations and structures. The information collected would be sent to the university's library so it would be accessible for future generations.

There was one story in particular while working on the gentrification project that really stuck out to her. It was the story of an older black couple who had been living in Athens since before the end of segregation. "They spoke of people refusing them service at convenience stores and being a part of historic sit-ins at a local restaurant," said Camryn.

Athens, as she discovered through her work on this project, was important historically, especially during the Civil Rights Movement. "That was kind of getting erased with football games and that kind of hoopla," she said about the town's history. Most of the students who attended the university were unaware of the history of Athens or the gentrification taking place there, and instead were only aware of the events happening directly at their school.

After helping with this project, Camryn was more aware of what was going on in her college town. "I try to stay more up to date with what's going on around me, especially because, well…I'm a part of the problem." She lives in an apartment in the city, so she is unintentionally contributing to gentrification. She now tries to stay more active at the local level so she can continue learning about what's going on in this city she lives in.

"I felt like it was my job to at least try to understand the issues of the local people who are majorly affected by my university. I have always seen homeless people and government housing on every corner, but I never even knew I lived in the poorest county in my state until getting involved in this project."

Now that Camryn has become involved with politics, she never wants to stop. She is working on a book, which she describes as "a memoir about racial identity and growing up in the twenty-first century." After graduation, she wants to get a job in public policy, potentially for a think tank. But she eventually wants to be a US Senator. She could also see herself starting at the local level, like she has done in college, by running for mayor and working her way up. As long as she gets to stay in Georgia politics, then what she ends up actually doing is less important.

"I know that I'm going to be in Georgia, because I feel like they need me here. If everyone leaves it will never change." Camryn is just a college student who wants to help her state and her community, and even though she didn't start getting involved until she was in college, she managed to create positive change in her community. Camryn provides an inspiring story for all of us.

According to a recent Public Religion Research Institute (PRRI) poll, 62 percent of Americans and 59 percent of young Americans surveyed believe that acting locally is more important than acting nationally.[85] Camryn, Lucy, Maya, and Pooja prove this is true. But this is true not just in the US Acting locally is a universally effective way to create change. Alessandra Orofino, in a 2014 TED Talk, tells us about an

---

85  Alex Vandermaas-Peeler et al., "American Democracy in Crisis: Civic Engagement, Young Adult Activism, and the 2018 Midterm Elections," Public Religion Research Institute, October 11, 2018.

organization she founded in her home city of Rio de Janeiro, Brazil. The organization is called Meu Rio, and it helps people organize around the local issues they care about. She provides, in this TED Talk, several success stories from the organization, but one story in particular really stuck with me.

"Amongst our members is this adorable little girl, Bia…Bia was just eleven years old when she started a campaign using one of our tools to save her model public school from demolition. Her school actually ranks among the best public schools in the country, and it was going to be demolished by the Rio de Janeiro state government to build—I kid you not—a parking lot for the World Cup right before the event happened. Bia started a campaign, and we even watched her school 24/7 through webcam monitoring, and many months afterward, the government changed their minds. Bia's school stayed in place."[86]

This story of an eleven-year-old girl in Brazil and the other stories shared in this chapter show us that getting involved early and locally are ways to affect a great deal of positive change. Whether you opt for high school or college clubs, local campaign work, non-profit work, or a little bit of everything, early and continued involvement is the best way to have an impact in your community. Local engagement is a great way to get a foot in the door and eventually move up the ladder to national politics.

---

86  Alessandra Orofino, "It's our city. Let's fix it," filmed October 2014 at TEDGlobal 2014, Video, 15:08.

# CHAPTER 6

# SPOT A PROBLEM AND FIND A SOLUTION

———

*The young, free to act on their initiative, can lead their elders in the direction of the unknown... The children, the young, must ask the questions that we would never think to ask.*

—MARGARET MEAD[87]

Emma Gonzalez was just eighteen years old when her life changed drastically. On February 14, 2018, a gunman opened fire in her high school, Marjory Stoneman Douglas High School in Parkland, Florida, killing seventeen people and injuring seventeen others. Luckily, she was not one of those thirty-four people, but some of her friends and classmates were.

———

87  Adam Fletcher, "Quotes about Youth + Social Change," Freechild Institute, January 28, 2020.

Unfortunately, Emma is far from the only person to ever be in this position. In 2018 alone, there were 340 mass shootings. 373 people died from mass shootings that year and over a thousand more were injured.[88] In 2019, there were 417 mass shootings, which is an average of more than one per day.[89] Emma is one of the countless numbers of people who have had their lives irreparably altered by gun violence. Few, however, have stood up and made their voices heard after a shooting as strongly as Emma did.

On February 17, three days after the Parkland shooting, Emma gave a speech at the Rally to Support Firearm Safety Legislation in Fort Lauderdale, Florida. "We are up here," she said at the beginning of the speech, "standing together because, if all our government and president can do is send 'thoughts and prayers,' then it's time for victims to be the change that we need to see." She spoke for eleven minutes and had to pause several times to allow for the thunderous applause of the crowd.

"The guns have changed and the laws have not," she said, reminding everyone of the problem. "We certainly do not understand why it should be harder to make plans with friends on weekends than it is to buy an automatic or semi-automatic weapon." Under Florida's gun laws at the time, people didn't need a permit or a license to buy or carry guns, so it was far too easy to get one.

---

88  Melia Robinson and Skye Gould, "There were 340 mass shootings in the US in 2018—here's the full list," *Business Insider,* December 31, 2018.

89  Jason Silverstein, "There were more mass shootings than days in 2019," *CBS News,* January 2, 2020.

Emma reminded everyone listening that mass shootings aren't really a problem in other countries. When the UK or Australia had a mass shooting, they passed gun control laws and didn't have another one. Emma expressed her frustration with the older generations' handling of the situation. "Maybe the adults have gotten used to saying 'it is what it is' but if us students have learned anything it's that if you don't study, you will fail, and in this case, if you actively do nothing, people continually end up dead. So, it's time to start doing something!"

She went on, in that speech, to specifically call out Congress, the NRA, and Donald Trump. She criticized Trump for telling her that it was a terrible tragedy and should never have happened, while still receiving thirty million dollars from the NRA.

"To every politician who is taking donations from the NRA, shame on you."

"Politicians who sit in their gilded House and Senate seats funded by the NRA, telling us that nothing could have ever been done to prevent this. We call BS! They say that tougher gun laws do not decrease violence. We call BS! They say a good guy with a gun stops a bad guy with a gun. We call BS! They say guns are just tools like knives and are as dangerous as cars. We call BS! They say that no laws could have been able to prevent the hundreds of senseless tragedies that have occurred. We call BS! That us kids don't know what we're talking about, that we're too young to understand how the government works. We call BS!"[90]

The crowd, by the end of the speech, was chanting "We call BS!" with her as she spoke.

Young people like Emma are uniquely situated to affect change because they can see the problems older people can't. They also aren't afraid to ask the tough questions and find the solutions. Emma saw the problem with current gun control regulations and went about figuring out how to fix it. She gave speeches, became active on social media, and even helped start a gun control advocacy group. She used her viewpoint as a young person—and the fact that gun control regulations would help prevent other young people from experiencing the same tragedy she herself experienced—to create change. In fact, because of her activism and the activism of other students at her school, gun control legislation was passed in Florida. The new law raises the purchase age to twenty-one and requires a three-day waiting period, among other things.[91] This legislation is not perfect, and we still have yet to see an expansion of national gun control laws, but it is a start, and it is largely due to Emma and her problem-solving.

Like Emma, many other people feel compelled to find solutions to problems after being affected by them directly. Mari Copeny was just eight years old in 2016 when she sent a letter to President Obama. In the letter, she asked the President if

---

90  "Florida student Emma Gonzalez to lawmakers and gun advocates: 'We call BS'," CNN, Updated February 17, 2018.

91  "Florida Gun Laws," Giffords Law Center, Accessed May 29, 2020.

she could meet with him during her upcoming trip to Washington, DC. She was going to DC, not for a school field trip or for a vacation, but because she was concerned about her hometown of Flint, Michigan. In 2014, the city switched its water supply from treated river and lake water to the Flint River in an effort to save money until they built a pipeline from Lake Huron. The Flint River had, for a very long time, been the unofficial waste disposal site for the city, so the water was extremely corrosive.[92] Since those in charge neglected to add corrosion inhibitors to the water, the water going to the citizens of Flint became infected with lead.

"My family, we were getting bad rashes, and headaches, eyes burning," said Mari about the water crisis.[93] By 2016, this lead contamination was so bad the governor of Michigan declared a state of emergency in Flint. He went to testify before Congress about it, which is what brought Mari and others from her town to the nation's capital.

"Little Miss Flint," as she called herself in her letter to him, didn't get to meet President Obama on that trip to DC, but she did get to meet him eventually. About a month and a half after her visit to the nation's capital—by which point Mari had given up hope of the President reading her letter—she received a response from him that said, "I am proud of you for using your voice to speak out on behalf of the children of Flint," and that he would be coming to Flint the following week and would love to meet her.

---

92  Melissa Denchak, "Flint Water Crisis: Everything You Need to Know," Natural Resources Defense Council, November 8, 2018.

93  "Future Women of America: Meet Mari Copeny," November 30, 2018, Brit + Co, video, 3:08.

He was true to his word. "Meeting Obama was so amazing. He gives the best hugs," Mari later said.[94] When the President gave a speech in Flint, he specifically mentioned Mari and said, "When something like this happens, a young girl shouldn't have to go to Washington to be heard" and that he thought he should come to Flint to meet with her instead.

It would have been very easy, after getting to meet the president, for her activism to stop there. But Mari didn't stop. Helping people was part of her nature so she wasn't going to just give up. "I started becoming an activist when I was four to, like, five. I started helping out with my grandmother, passing out food to people who couldn't afford food, so we just gave them food for free." Because she had been helping people for so long, it felt only natural she would keep this activism going. She began raising money for clean water, but also for school supplies, toys, and other things that would benefit the children of Flint.

"I wanted to speak up and say, 'Hey, the water's bad. Can someone please fix it?' but they never did fix it," she said. At the height of the crisis, the water contamination was so bad that it actually doubled the prevalence of high blood lead levels in children, so Mari, a child herself, had to take things into her own hands.[95]

The government is slowly fixing the situation and is in the process of replacing the lead service lines in the city, but many people are still getting their water from these bad

---

94  Ibid.
95  Denchak, "Flint Water Crisis."

pipes.[96] When the government stopped paying for bottled waters for the city in 2018, Mari began raising money and, along with a huge team of people, began distributing cases of water to people. "The government stopped paying for our water so now people have to buy it," she said. "So, we decided we should just give them water."[97] Since people were using bottled water for everything—drinking, cooking, even brushing their teeth—families like Mari's are using three cases of water a day. This is unsustainable, especially for low-income families, so it's a big deal that she is helping provide free water.

Since 2016, Mari has raised over five hundred thousand dollars for the children of Flint, and she isn't stopping there. She has recently switched from providing water bottles—which is not very environmentally friendly—to attempting to provide water filters not just to Flint, but to communities all over the US that are dealing with toxic water.[98]

Mari Copeny's story shows us you're never too young to solve problems and make a difference in your community. As her sister put it in a 2018 interview, "Age is just a number—an eight-year-old girl got the President of the United States to come to Flint, Michigan. As long as you're determined and very outspoken, then you can do it all."[99]

---

96   Ibid.

97   "Meet Mari Copeny," Brit + Co.

98   "About Mari," on Mari Copeny's official website, Accessed May 29, 2020.

99   "Meet Mari Copeny," Brit + Co.

Mari, with that letter to President Obama, and with the letter writing project she started to send positive messages to kids in Flint, forced the federal government to pay attention to her small town and to the problems it was facing. She continues to be a positive force for change in Flint and around the country and continues to inspire other kids to be activists in their community. In her acceptance speech at the Shorty Awards, where she won the award for Best in Activism for her use of social media to promote her clean water campaign, Mari offered this powerful reminder: "To all the kids out there, listen, if they refuse you, if they refuse to give you a seat at the table, stand on it with a megaphone and make them listen to you."[100]

## ASK TOUGH QUESTIONS

Greta Thunberg, a seventeen-year-old activist from Sweden, began making international headlines when she skipped school to push the Swedish Parliament for action on climate change. She held up a sign that said "School strike for the climate" and spent her day outside Parliament every day for almost a month. She has now traveled all over the world, led climate strikes, and given speeches about this issue that means so much to her.

Greta first heard about climate change when she was just eight years old. "I remember thinking that it was very strange that humans, who are an animal species among others, could

---

100 "Mari Copeny WINS Best in Activism || Shorty Awards 2019," May 6, 2019, Shorty Awards, video, 2:50.

be capable of changing the Earth's climate. Because if we were, and if it was really happening, we wouldn't be talking about anything else," she said. "But no one ever talked about it. If burning fossil fuels was so bad that it threatened our very existence, how could we just continue like before? Why were there no restrictions? Why wasn't it made illegal?"

She couldn't understand why no one else seemed to be worried about climate change, and why no one was in a rush to take action. This, she felt, was a big deal, and it seemed strange that very few people seemed to care.

A few years later, she became depressed and stopped eating and talking. She was diagnosed with Asperger's, OCD, and selective mutism. Selective mutism, as she describes it, means, "I only speak when I think it's necessary." But these diagnoses did not stop her from advocating for climate change. She pushed for her parents to make changes in their lifestyle to reduce the family's carbon footprint; for example, she wanted them to become vegan and to stop flying in airplanes. There was initially resistance from her family, but that didn't stop her from continuing her fight.

In August of 2018, when Greta was just fifteen years old, she began her school climate strikes. She skipped school and stood outside the Swedish Parliament every day until September 9 when Sweden held its general election. She wanted Sweden to reduce its carbon emissions because it was not meeting the requirements of the Paris Climate Agreement, which requires every country that signs with it to reduce greenhouse gas emissions in an effort to limit global rise in temperature.[101]

"Some people say that I should be in school instead," said Greta. "Some people say that I should study to become a climate scientist so that I can 'solve the climate crisis'. But the climate crisis has already been solved. We already have all the facts and solutions. All we have to do is to wake up and change."

After the election, she reduced her strike to only Fridays and attended school all the other days. She posted a photo of her strike on social media and after the photo was shared by reporters, companies, and other social media accounts, she started gaining international recognition. She began traveling around Europe, participating in demonstrations, and giving speeches.

In November of 2018, Greta gave a TED talk in Stockholm.[102] She finally had an answer to the question of why no one has done anything to fix climate change.

"People keep doing what they do because the vast majority doesn't have a clue about the actual consequences of our everyday life, and they don't know that rapid change is required. We all think we know, and we all think everybody knows, but we don't." She painted a rather grim picture of the future, saying, "What we do or don't do right now will affect

---

101 "The Paris Agreement," Process and meetings, United Nations Framework Convention on Climate Change, Accessed May 29, 2020.

102 Greta Thunberg, "The disarming case to act right now on climate change," filmed November 2018 at TEDxStockholm, Video, 11:04.

my entire life and the lives of my children and grandchildren. What we do or don't do right now, me and my generation can't undo in the future."

In September 2019, she traveled overseas—in an environmentally friendly boat, of course, since flying would have contributed to the carbon footprint—to attend the UN Climate Action Summit in New York City. In the speech she gave at the event, she called out everyone who refused to do anything about climate change. "People are suffering. People are dying. Entire ecosystems are collapsing. We are in the beginning of a mass extinction and all you can talk about is money and fairy tales of eternal economic growth. How dare you!" She went around North America, participating in climate protests in Canada and the US.

She left the US with these parting words: "My message to the Americans is the same as to everyone; that is to unite behind the science and to act on the science."

Greta is remarkably strong and resilient, especially considering how much criticism of her efforts there has been and how many people have attacked her. Donald Trump has tweeted about her multiple times, saying after she was chosen to be TIME's Person of the Year in 2019, "Greta must work on her anger management problem, then go to a good old-fashioned movie with a friend! Chill Greta, Chill!"[103]

---

103 Derrick Bryson Taylor, "Trump Mocks Greta Thunberg on Twitter, and She Jabs Back," *The New York Times,* December 12, 2019.

But Greta didn't let his words get to her, and had a snarky response by changing her Twitter bio to read, "A teenager working on her anger management problem. Currently chilling and watching a good old-fashioned movie with a friend."[104] This was not the first time she reacted this way; the first time Trump attacked her on Twitter, she also responded by changing her bio to twist his words around. Countless other people have attacked her for being so vocal about climate change, but she never lets anyone's words bring her down. She just keeps on fighting for this issue she cares about.

What can we learn from Greta's story? Her words teach us that actions—or lack thereof—have consequences. If we do not take action on climate change, and even if we ourselves do not feel the consequences, we will be hurting future generations. Greta has shown us that the older generations will not necessarily make the best choices for the younger generation.

"You are failing us, but the young people are starting to understand your betrayal. The eyes of all future generations are upon you, and if you choose to fail us, I say, we will never forgive you."

Climate change may not affect the older generations, but it will certainly affect the younger ones. Millennials and Generation Z will feel the effects of climate change and the lack of action by the older generations. Greta Thunberg has inspired what is called "the Greta effect": young people all over the world are following in her footsteps and taking action. They are beginning to realize their actions can have an impact and

104 Ibid.

the policy decisions made by legislatures have consequences. So, it is up to the young people, people like Greta Thunberg, to remind the older generations the future is at stake here and their actions directly affect us.

Greta Thunberg is not the only kid asking adults the tough questions. Sophie Cruz was just five years old on September 23, 2015, when she broke through a barricade to deliver a letter to the Pope. Sophie, who was living in Los Angeles, California, at the time, had traveled all the way to Washington, DC, with her parents and a group called the Catholic Delegation for Reform just to see Pope Francis. In her letter, she asked Pope Francis to help her parents.

Sophie herself is a US citizen but she is the daughter of two undocumented immigrants from Oaxaca, Mexico. She was asking for the Pope's help that day because she was "scared that one day ICE is going to deport my parents," as she stated in her letter. She wanted his help in saving DAPA (Deferred Action for Parents of Americans), which would allow her parents to remain in the United States legally. Pope Francis stopped the parade to hug her, and he later read the letter she wrote him.

"Immigrants like my dad feed this country," she said in the letter, pleading her case. "They therefore deserve to live with dignity, they deserve to be respected, they deserve immigration reform, because it would be beneficial to my country, and because they have earned it working very hard, picking oranges, onions, watermelons, spinach, lettuce, and many other vegetables." She called for his help in making sure that she and others like her would not be separated from their parents.

"I have a right to live with my parents. I have a right to be happy...Don't forget about us, the children."[105]

The day after he hugged Sophie during the parade, the Pope had a meeting scheduled with the US Congress. In this meeting, he brought up immigration reform, telling Congress it should be more welcoming of immigrants and refugees. Sophie singlehandedly influenced the Pope's talking points by handing him that letter, which is quite remarkable for someone so young.

Her activism didn't stop there. She continued to be an advocate for immigration reform and immigrants' rights and Americans paid attention. In 2016, she was invited to the White House to celebrate Cinco de Mayo with President Obama and Vice President Biden. Later that same year, she submitted a question for one of the presidential debates, asking what would happen to her if her parents were deported. Although the question was never aired, it shows a remarkable amount of courage and commitment to her cause that she wanted to ask the future president a tough question. Also, in 2016, Sophie and her family were featured in a short film in which they talked about how DAPA would help them all stay together. This film premiered at the Tribeca Film Festival that year.

---

105 Danielli, "Meet 8-Year-Old Latina Immigration Activist Sophie Cruz Who Is Changing The Conversation On Immigrant Rights," *mitú*, March 21, 2019.

In January of 2017, Sophie gave a speech at the Women's March on Washington. She stood up on stage with her parents and her younger sister, holding the microphone and giving her speech in both English and Spanish. "We are here together making a chain of love to protect our families," she said during her speech. It was clear from this speech what mattered most to her: protecting families and spreading the love. "Let us fight with love, faith, and courage so that our families will not be destroyed."

To all the children listening, she offered this message of hope and strength: "I also want to tell the children not to be afraid, because we are not alone. Still many people have their hearts filled with love and tender to snuggle in this path of life. Let's keep together and fight for our rights!"[106]

This little girl who spoke both English and Spanish in front of a crowd of half a million people was quite inspiring to people and, in fact, is still one of the faces of the immigration reform movement. People on the Internet have created artwork with her face with empowering slogans on it. In 2018, the San Jose Museum of Art began displaying a mural with her face on it, called "Sophie Holding the World Together." The museum's description of this mural calls Sophie a "symbol of resolve and hope; a coming together across borders to fight for a shared future."[107] She, like this mural, inspires people and gives them hope that someday there will be immigration reform.

---

106 Mary Bowerman, "Watch: 6-year-old Sophie Cruz captures hearts at massive Women's March," *USA Today*, January 21, 2017.

107 San Jose Museum of Art, "A Mural of Hope," Accessed June 25, 2020.

It really is quite remarkable how large of an impact Sophie has had on the US political landscape. She didn't know, when she first set out to give Pope Francis that letter, she would be inspiring so many people, she just knew she didn't want her parents to be deported. But she spoke up for what she wanted, she asked tough questions, and she sought solutions. Even though she was quite young, people listened. In 2018, Define American, which tries to change the narrative about immigration and citizenship in the US, named her its "activist of the year," and the county of Los Angeles awarded her a commendation for her activism. Today, at just nine years old, she continues to be a positive voice for change. At the rate she's going, she's likely to accomplish some amazing things by the time she's old enough to vote.

## SEE THINGS THROUGH

One of the biggest lessons I learned in my childhood was, "If at first you don't succeed, try, try again." My parents and teachers and even peers would say that to me, and it's still the phrase that goes through my head whenever I get discouraged. And trust me, I've had my fair share of failures; I've run for officer positions I didn't win, I've applied for scholarships and awards I didn't win, and I've applied to many internships I didn't get. But, despite all of these failures, I have always kept trying.

Now, I realize this example is cheesy and seems too simple for a book about politics, but this lesson has more relevance than you would think. In fact, I think it is particularly relevant in politics. Even if you don't succeed the first time, you should "try, try again." If you keep fighting for what you believe in, eventually you will succeed.

Cassandra Levesque is a perfect example of this. Cassandra is a newly elected member of the New Hampshire House of Representatives. Like all of the other 399 members of the New Hampshire House, she had to be elected by the constituents of her district. Like everyone else, she takes her seat every morning and does her best to represent her district. Like everyone else, she votes on policy and sits in committee.

But Cassandra Levesque is not like everyone else.

For starters, she is only nineteen, making her the youngest member of the New Hampshire legislature. And in a legislature with an average age of sixty-six, that makes a difference—not to mention the legislature is almost 70 percent male, which makes Cassandra even more impressive.[108] But how did she get here? What brought her to run for office? Why should we care?

It started, believe it or not, with a Girl Scout project. When Cassandra was seventeen, as her Girl Scout Gold Award project, she began working to try and end child marriage in New Hampshire. At the time, the legal age to marry was thirteen for girls and fourteen for boys. Her inspiration for tackling this problem came from "my research and from my

---

108 "Women in State Legislatures for 2019," Women's Legislative Network, National Conference of State Legislatures, July 25, 2019.

family ancestry," she said, "and seeing that child marriage is happening in my family."[109]

Child marriage is not just a problem in New Hampshire. In fact, it is legal in all but two states, and almost 250,000 children got married in the United States alone between 2000 and 2010. All that is needed in a lot of these states is parental permission, which means this often happens against the child's will.[110] Cassandra worked with New Hampshire Representative Jacalyn Cilley, who, with Cassandra's help, sponsored a bill that would raise the legal marriage age to eighteen in New Hampshire.

But this wasn't as easy as it appeared to be, and Cassandra's bill faced a lot of backlash from legislators. People were concerned about teens who were deployed for military service; typically, only spouses have any rights if anything happens, so being legally married is very important for military couples. The bill Cassandra initially proposed didn't pass primarily because of this.

She could have chosen to stop there and drop this issue as soon as she received her Gold Award. After all, she had put up a valiant fight and had come really close. Isn't that what mattered?

109 "New Hampshire State Rep. Cassie Levesque Wants To End Child Marriage," November 26, 2018, NowThis, produced by Jackie Padilla, video, 2:42.

110 Daniele Selby, "Child Marriage is Legal in the US. How You Can Help End it," Global Citizen, September 3, 2019.

It wasn't enough for Cassandra, however. "It didn't make me want to stop. It just made me want to push forward," she said about her initial failure.[111] She continued to advocate for this issue, and with Representative Cilley's help, the legislature raised the marriage age to sixteen.

It seemed as though that was the end of Cassandra's advocacy in the state House of Representatives because she left town to study photography at the New Hampshire Institute of Art. But she soon realized she did not want a career in photography and returned to her hometown. She later enrolled in online classes at Southern New Hampshire University as a political science student.

Shortly after returning home, she was approached by another state representative, Ellen Read, who had co-sponsored Cassandra's bill. Representative Read asked her to run for a vacant seat in the New Hampshire House of Representatives. "I never really thought I would be into politics," said Cassandra. "I was an arts student."[112] She went back and forth on whether to run and finally, right before the deadline, she filed her papers and entered the race.

Cassandra had to beat out four other candidates to win the race, which was by no means an easy task. But for a former Girl Scout, going door-to-door campaigning and talking to people was no big deal. "What was more scary was asking people for money, even though I already did that with

---

111  Kate Taylor, "In New Class of Young Lawmakers, a Former Girl Scout Goes to the Statehouse," *The New York Times*, November 13, 2018.

112  Bre Bradham, "Q&A: Young politicians explain what it's like being college-aged elected officials," *The Chronicle*, March 6, 2019.

cookies," she said.[113] But by utilizing social media—posting on Twitter and Facebook asking for three-dollar donations—she gained a lot of followers and received a lot of donations. And living in a town where everybody knows everybody made it much easier to spread her message.

Somehow, at just nineteen years old, she won the race and got to take her seat in the New Hampshire House. She thinks her age had a lot to do with this victory. The advantage that being young provides her is "helping people and other representatives understand, 'Hey, this is what the youth wants, this is what we all want to do to make New Hampshire better,'" she says.[114]

Now that she is in the legislature, Cassandra is going to try again to get the marriage age raised to eighteen. Since the last time she tried this, she has done some research and now feels more confident she can get it done. The first time around, she shared, "I felt very nervous because I didn't know anybody," but now, "I know the people on the committee, I have relationships with other legislators. Now, I'm confident in what I know, I have facts. I have a six-inch binder just full of data."[115] She feels much more prepared for criticism and questions this time, especially for questions about teens in the military. She has looked into it, and whether or not these teens are married will not affect their survivor benefits. Cassandra is hoping she can use that to garner support for the bill.

---

113  Ibid.

114  Beth Germano, "19-Year-Old Ready To Become Youngest New Hampshire Lawmaker," CBS Boston, November 27, 2018.

115  Leah Willingham, "Now a legislator, Girl Scout returns to State House to raise marriage age to 18," *Concord Monitor*, February 19, 2019.

"For a seventeen-year-old girl who is marrying willingly and for all the right reasons, waiting a few months to marry is at worst an inconvenience," she said.[116] The main reason to raise the age to eighteen is to protect those who are forced into child marriages.

She says she has heard from victims of child marriages. "They have shared their stories with me. Their voices will forever echo in my heart and mind."[117] This bill is her way of giving a voice to the voiceless and preventing them from being forced into marrying too young.

Though ending child marriage is still her primary goal, Cassandra also wants to focus on raising the minimum wage and figuring out ways to bring more young people to New Hampshire. "I'm more focused on trying to do more activism and getting girls' voices heard," she said in an interview with NowThis.[118] "I will always stick to my gut and what I feel is right."

Why should we care that she's doing all of this? By being the youngest member of an extremely old and male-dominated legislature, she's helping provide a voice for those who have been silenced and speaking on behalf of the younger generations in her state.

---

116  Ibid.

117  Ibid.

118  "New Hampshire State Rep. Cassie Levesque Wants To End Child Marriage," November 26, 2018, NowThis, produced by Jackie Padilla, video, 2:42.

"It's really empowering and exciting to see what's next for the youth movement, this wave of youth going through politics and being heard," she said. "It feels really great. I can bring more of a voice of the youth in the New Hampshire House by bringing up laws or just talking to people."[119]

Cassandra saw a problem in her state and figured out how to fix it and by doing so, she realized a person who had no experience or prior interest in politics could still make a positive change in their community and provide a voice to the voiceless.

Cassandra Levesque, Emma Gonzalez, Mari Copeny, Sophie Cruz, and Greta Thunberg all show us that identifying problems and figuring out how to solve them is a very effective way to make a difference as a young person in politics. Young people are the future and can identify problems that the older generations cannot. This makes them ideally suited to affect change in big ways. The brave young women in this chapter have tackled a variety of problems and have demonstrated that hard work and creative problem-solving can lead to so much positive change.

---

119  Germano, "Youngest New Hampshire Lawmaker."

# CHAPTER 7

# TAKE OPPORTUNITIES WHERE YOU FIND THEM

---

*Opportunities, many times, are so small that we glimpse yet they are often the seeds of great enterprises. Opportunities are also everywhere and so you must always let your hook be hanging. When you least expect it, a great fish will swim by.*

—OG MANDINO[120]

My freshman year of college, I was offered the opportunity to go to the state legislature in Richmond one day and lobby on behalf of the school. I had never done anything like that before, but I decided to go anyway. While in Richmond, I went to legislators' offices to speak to them about the various higher education bills being considered in the legislature that year. As a student at a public university, this legislation would have directly affected me and my classmates.

---

120 "13 Quotes to Motivate You to Seize Opportunities," SUCCESS Staff, SUCCESS, May 2, 2019.

This experience ended up being extremely valuable for me. It put me outside my comfort zone and gave me the opportunity to speak up on behalf of the school I love so much. I got the chance to speak directly with legislators as well as with other important people in the Virginia legislature at a reception we attended that evening. Both of those were an invaluable experience for me.

My junior year, when I signed up for this same program, I was given the opportunity to go to Richmond earlier in the day and get a tour of the Governor's Mansion by the First Lady of Virginia. I expected a lot of people to sign up for that experience, but only a few did. Because there were so few of us, we got a very personalized tour and the opportunity to have some really important conversations with the First Lady of Virginia. I even got to take a photo with her!

That important experience gave me the chance to feel like my voice was being heard by someone in charge. It was an opportunity I never expected to get and I am extremely grateful I took it even though it put me outside my comfort zone.

My story and the stories to follow in this chapter provide a very important lesson: Take opportunities as they arise, even if they seem scary or like they won't align with your ultimate career goals. Often, the surprising opportunities are what lead to real change or a rediscovered passion for something.

Allison Greenday had just graduated college when she became a field organizer for Democrat Dan Helmer's campaign for the Virginia House of Delegates. This meant she did a lot of canvassing and speaking with potential voters.

Becoming a field organizer was not something she had anticipated doing right after college, but taking this opportunity ended up paying off for her in the long run.

After Helmer won the race, he offered Allison a job as a legislative aide during the upcoming legislative session. This was an opportunity she had not anticipated, but she took the job anyway. As a legislative aide, she has been given the chance to witness the legislative process and have a say in what happens. She has gotten to witness great progress being made. For example, Virginia finally passed the Equal Rights Amendment, which protects against discrimination on the basis of sex. This bill had been under consideration for many years in Virginia, so getting it passed was a huge step forward for women. As a legislative aide, Allison got to be part of the process. If she had not taken the opportunity to become a legislative aide when it was presented to her, then she might not have been able to witness history being made with the ratification of the Equal Rights Amendment.

Since the General Assembly's session ended in March, Allison now has to look for new ways to get involved and serve the public. She might stay in campaigns and administrative roles, but she could also see herself doing research or even going into the bureaucracy. "The main issue for me is I just want to find…a platform where I can do the most, whatever that ends up being," she said. So she is open to going wherever life takes her next, seizing any opportunities thrown her way and working wherever she can have the greatest impact on her community.

To those wanting to follow in her footsteps, Allison offers this advice: "Be willing to pay your dues, be willing to put in the hard work, because the hard work is the most gratifying. The hard work is how you know you're making a difference." Yes, campaign work might be grueling and exhausting, but it is also rewarding and a great entryway into the world of politics. When you put in the kind of hard work Allison did as a field organizer, you can actually see the effects of your actions. Because of the campaigning Allison and others did for their candidates, Democrats were able to take control of both houses in the Virginia legislature, giving them the power to affect real and meaningful change in the state.

But the most important advice Allison can give is this: "Go after what you want. Be explicit and direct about it. If you don't ask for what you want, if you don't, kind of, take it, then don't expect people to offer it to you. You need to be clear with your own boundaries, clear with what you want. And even if it seems like a long shot—like, if it means going up to the campaign manager at the end of the campaign and asking them to help connect you with high-level positions moving forward—do it. People will work with you, people will help you…find that support system."

Allison's story shows us we should be taking opportunities where we find them, even if they seem minor, as they can lead to so much positive change in our communities. She could not have guessed when she accepted the job as a field organizer that she would eventually be witnessing the passage of the Equal Rights Amendment.

## OPPORTUNITY LEADS TO CHANGE

Not only did Pooja Tanjore serve as the Virginia State Director of Rise to Run, but she also co-started a humanitarian organization in high school and served as chair of an international youth summit. She graduated from high school a year early and took a gap year as a junior ambassador to Germany before starting college at William & Mary. She has attended several prestigious summer programs and has been interviewed several times, including an interview with Scholastic about the 2016 election. Overall, she is extremely impressive, especially since she is only nineteen and a freshman in college.

But how did she get here? Is this something we could all do or does Pooja have something special?

Apparently it all started with a tweet. "It sort of began with me tweeting Rise to Run and being like, 'Oh, I love you guys,'" Pooja told me in an interview. "And then they DMed me back and they were like 'Well, where are you from?' and I was like, 'Well, I'm from Virginia and…I have a lot of organizing experience. I love what you guys do.'" After that, they offered her a job, and the rest is history.

But there's more to the story than that. Pooja has always been really invested in helping others. "Civic engagement and helping people has always been…inherently part of who I am. It was never really a question of 'Am I going to be helping the people that need to be helped?' It was always just sort of default. I always knew that was where I belonged."

But she never meant to make a career out of it. In fact, she didn't know you *could* make a career out of helping people. When Pooja first started getting involved in politics, she was motivated only by her desire to "ensure that those in politics have lived our experiences" by fighting for more proportional representation in government.

She soon realized her actions had a real impact. "It was feasible to help other people, and it was most effective to help other people through policy," she said in an interview for a podcast.[121] After that initial Twitter exchange with Rise to Run, she started their Northern Virginia chapter and began to travel all over the state, talking to local high schools and encouraging girls to get involved in politics. The Virginia branch of Rise to Run eventually included twenty-two schools across the state. This growth is due largely in part to Pooja, who managed to run the organization even after she moved to Germany the following year.

What can we learn from Pooja's story and from Rise to Run? The main lesson is anyone can do this; you don't have to be a certain kind of person to get involved in politics and make a difference in your community. Pooja is a prime example of someone who was given an opportunity to affect change, took it, and is now able to see the positive effects of her actions.

"I think a lot of people feel like they have to be super educated or be perfect to be involved, but that's just not the case. Like, you can go in blind—I'm not saying run for president, with

---

121  Melissa Currence and Amy Hjerstedt, "Episode 18: Young Leader in Her Own Words," July 7, 2018, in *What Would Alice Paul Do?*, podcast, 25:14.

no experience, but I am saying go try something new." Take the opportunities you are given, even if they are completely different from anything you've done before, and even if you feel underqualified, because they can lead to positive change in your community.

In her TED Talk, Kare Anderson describes a similar phenomenon. In this lecture, she calls on everyone to become "opportunity-makers": to seek the opportunity to work with others to accomplish something greater. She says opportunity-makers have three main traits: They "keep honing their top strength and they become pattern seekers. They get involved in different worlds than their worlds so they're trusted and they can see those patterns, and they communicate to connect around sweet spots of shared interest."[122]

The main takeaway from Anderson is the idea that seizing opportunities, and in fact, creating your own opportunities, can lead to positive change. Going outside your comfort zone, interacting with people with different interests, and working together on something can have a real impact and lead to further opportunities. Although Anderson isn't talking specifically about politics, this is a message that applies to all fields; politics included. Work across the aisle and with people that have different beliefs, and never be afraid to take advantage of an opportunity that presents itself. Opportunity leads to change, so take the opportunities you are given or create your own opportunities to make a difference.

---

122 Kare Anderson, "Be an opportunity maker," filmed September 2014 at TED@IBM, Video, 9:38.

## OPPORTUNITY LEADS TO FULFILLMENT

For me, an opportunity to affect change presented itself last summer. My friend Lucy texted me one day and said she was working for a candidate who was running in the primary for the Virginia House of Delegates. She said the campaign needed some people to come canvass for them a few times and they would pay people for it.

As a college student who was in desperate need of money, I agreed to come canvass the weekend before the election. It was, as are most canvassing jobs, grueling and a bit frustrating. And since it was June in Northern Virginia, it was quite hot and humid outside. I also distinctly remember it raining on at least one of the four days I was canvassing.

Although canvassing was tough, it was extremely fulfilling. On the night of the election, I was checking the results and saw the candidate I had supported won. The feeling of learning all my hard work paid off and the four days I had spent outside in the heat weren't for nothing was an incredible and indescribable feeling. It felt so rewarding to know I had made a difference and helped him get elected, even if I had only worked for him for four days. I had taken this job primarily because I needed money but it led to me feeling extremely fulfilled and wanting to do even more to get involved in politics. It was an opportunity I almost passed up, and I'm glad I didn't.

Lucy Greenman, the friend who got me the canvassing job, actually had a very similar story. The school year prior to that summer, she had been working on a federal House campaign for Representative Jennifer Wexton. After the campaign was a success and Wexton won the election, Lucy started college and moved on with her life. Her political involvement could have ended there; after all, she did what she set out to do, which was help oust her representative who she didn't think represented her very well. But in January of the following year, when she attended now-Representative Wexton's inauguration party, she met the campaign manager of a candidate running for the Virginia House of Delegates. The campaign manager gave Lucy her email, and in early May of the same year, while Lucy was still at school, she got an email from the woman offering her a job.

The candidate was Suhas Subramanyam, and he was running in a Democratic primary against three other candidates. For this campaign, Lucy was a field organizer, which meant she spent most of her time canvassing, knocking on people's doors, and talking to them. Thanks to the efforts of Lucy and the others working on this campaign, Suhas won the four-way primary with 47 percent of the vote, which was more than double what the second-place candidate got. A large part of his success was likely due to the sheer number of people they talked to. According to Lucy, they knocked on about fifty thousand doors before the primary, which is an insanely high amount, considering the district only has about seventy thousand voters.[123]

After working on two campaigns, Lucy has learned it's the little things that make it all worth it. "The tedium behind the

---

123 "House of Delegates District 87," Virginia Public Access Project, Accessed June 1, 2020.

scenes is just so necessary," she said. Canvassing was pretty miserable, considering how hot it was, how many doors she knocked, and how few of the people at those doors actually wanted to talk to her.

"But then we got completely unprecedented voter turnout for a delegate primary, and we swept our four-way race so, I mean, it's those little things that really matter."

Lucy's story shows us that taking opportunities where you find them, even when they are completely unexpected, can lead to a very fulfilling experience. Lucy didn't go looking for a job as a field organizer, but she ended up loving it anyway and feeling very fulfilled after seeing what she could help accomplish. Her story, as well as Allison's and Pooja's, show us that, though these opportunities may involve a lot of hard work, they can make a huge difference in shaping the political landscape in our communities.

So, I offer this advice to you: Take the opportunities presented to you. Apply for jobs if they look interesting, even if you don't think they align with your ultimate career goals. Go try new things when the opportunity presents itself. You might just find you can change your community for the better, and you might even find you really enjoy it!

# CHAPTER 8

# USE SOCIAL MEDIA

———

*When you give everyone a voice and give people power, the system usually ends up in a really good place.*

—MARK ZUCKERBERG[124]

Mari Copeny is a young activist who began getting involved in politics when her hometown of Flint, Michigan began having problems with its water. She helped bring national attention to the Flint water crisis and to her clean water campaign, which involved providing water bottles to families so they could have clean water to use. In addition to this clean water campaign, in 2018, Mari started the Dear Flint Kids Project. With this program, she asked people all over the world to send her letters with positive messages, which she distributed to kids in Flint. The idea behind the project was to let kids know they are more than just victims of this water crisis. She received many letters from people all over the

---

124 Silvia Pencak, "Top 50+ Social Media Quotes," Powerful Life Consulting, Accessed June 1, 2020.

country, due in large part to the fact she used social media, specifically Twitter, to advertise the project.

The Dear Flint Kids Project wasn't the only thing Mari has successfully used social media for. She also used it to advertise her clean water campaign, and people noticed. In 2019, Mari won the Shorty Award, which honors the effective use of social media for activism. She was nominated alongside Colin Kaepernick, Jameela Jamil, and other impressive, well-established people. "I never thought that I would win activist," she said in her acceptance speech. "I was just a kid that was out to save my city that has now been without clean water for five years."[125]

As Mari's story shows us, social media can be a powerful tool in politics, both as a means by which to spread a message and as a tool with which to stay informed about current events. Social media has risen to prominence in the last ten years, and it is now widely used, especially by the younger generations, for both social and professional purposes.

In a 2009 TED Talk, Clay Shirky described the three main effects social media has had on the ways we communicate. The first change is media now supports conversations from many to many. Traditional media gave us the "one to many" system, and early telephones gave us the "one to one" system, but with social media, there is the potential for groups and conversation at the same time. The second change is that, as Shirky described, all media migrates to the Internet

---

125 "Mari Copeny WINS Best in Activism || Shorty Awards 2019," May 6, 2019, Shorty Awards, video, 2:50.

and thus becomes a site of coordination rather than a fountain of information. The third change is consumers are now also producers. This means those who previously were just consuming information can now respond and make their voices heard as well.[126] These changes have altered the ways we communicate, both about politics and about everyday occurrences.

Though all forms of social media can be utilized in various ways, the two primary social media platforms used in politics in the present day are Twitter and Facebook. On Twitter, people only have 280 characters to use when they tweet. If they want to type longer tweets, they'll have to break it into two tweets and reply to their original tweet. Retweeting something is a way of saying you agree with something or you think something is funny. Politicians typically use retweets to signal their endorsement of a message.

But beyond retweets, politicians can use the platform to engage with their constituents. They can tweet out a stance on a policy and see who replies to their tweet, they can quote someone else's tweet—quoting is essentially retweeting but with additional commentary—or they can create polls to gauge their followers' interests. Outside of use by politicians to engage with their constituents, Twitter can be an effective tool in public policy because it allows people to call out factual errors or make their ideas heard by the public.

---

126 Clay Shirky, "How social media can make history," filmed June 2009 at TED@State, Video, 15:33.

Facebook is used by politicians in a variety of ways. Like Twitter, it can be useful for engaging with constituents. When a politician makes a post, users have the option to react to it (like, love, sad react, wow react, and angry react are the five options), comment on it, or share it. All of these options give people the opportunity to make their thoughts heard on the issue and interact with their politicians. Facebook is typically the preferred platform for older people, whereas younger generations tend to migrate toward Twitter and Snapchat.

Instagram has also been growing in popularity as a political platform. Instagram used to be primarily for sharing photos, but since the creation of Instagram stories—a place where people can post something or share someone else's post and it goes away after twenty-four hours—this has increasingly become a platform for activism.

The example that springs to mind here is the support for the Black Lives Matter movement after the deaths of George Floyd and many other Black people at the hands of white police officers. People used their Instagram stories as a way to spread information on how to fight against racism and to show support for the Black community. June 2, 2020 was also deemed Blackout Tuesday, where people posted a black square on their Instagram feed as a way to show solidarity.[127]

I myself have used various social media platforms to promote my own political ideas. Though I don't use Twitter very much, I have found it to be a very good tool for activism. When a

---

127 Noah Manskar, "What is 'Blackout Tuesday'? Trend floods social media amid George Floyd protests," *New York Post,* June 2, 2020.

politician or activist posts something I really like, I'll retweet it so it also appears on my friends' feeds, and if a politician says something I really disagree with, I'll quote the tweet and add in my contrasting opinion. By doing this, I always hope someone will read it and be persuaded by my argument. I also occasionally use Snapchat or my Instagram story to show support for a movement or advertise my political beliefs.

However, the most common way I use social media is by adding a temporary profile picture on Facebook with a frame that either supports a political movement or encourages people to vote for a certain candidate. I also sometimes post on Facebook with the link to the Virginia Department of Elections' voter registration page, reminding people of the deadline and encouraging them to register to vote, or to order their absentee ballots.

Perhaps the most famous recent example of social media's importance is the story of Representative Alexandria Ocasio-Cortez. AOC made history on November 6, 2018, when she became the youngest woman ever elected to Congress. Born in 1989 to a Puerto Rican mother and a father from the Bronx, she never intended to go into politics. She grew up in the suburbs of New York City and has lived in or near the city almost her whole life. Until she declared her candidacy, she was just a working-class New Yorker, employed at a restaurant, living paycheck to paycheck and trying to pay off her student debt.

"Women like me aren't supposed to run for office," she later said in a campaign ad. "I wasn't born to a wealthy or powerful family."[128] Her parents were ordinary New Yorkers and she knew running for political office was something that only those with money or status did. While at Boston University, she had the opportunity to intern in Senator Ted Kennedy's office, in the foreign affairs and immigration division, where she learned more about the US Immigration and Customs Enforcement (ICE) and the trauma it can cause people. In fact, when she ran for office, the abolition of ICE became part of her platform.

Later, in 2016, she worked as an organizer for Bernie Sanders' presidential campaign. After the election, she traveled around the US speaking to people about the issues affecting their hometowns. It was on this trip she really felt inspired to get involved in politics and help her community, despite not being born into the wealth or power most candidates seemed to have.

In 2018, when Ocasio-Cortez declared she would be challenging Joe Crowley—who had held New York's 14th District in the House of Representatives for almost ten years—the world was shocked.

"My campaign is challenging Joseph Crowley, one of the most corporate-funded members of Congress, on an entirely progressive and grassroots campaign," she declared, launching a campaign whose mission was to fight back against the idea that only those with money or who are renowned can

---

128 "The Courage to Change | Alexandria Ocasio-Cortez," May 30, 2018, Alexandria Ocasio-Cortez, video, 2:08.

be involved in politics.[129] "When you said that you're going to take on Joe Crowley, I mean, people looked at you like you were crazy," a reporter told her in an interview. "I mean, you're going up against the Queens machine, as they call it."

"Yeah, yeah, but you know what? We meet a machine with a movement."[130] Ocasio-Cortez's "movement" was a movement to create "a government of the people, by the people, and for the people," in true American fashion. And just like in 1863, when those famous words were spoken by Abraham Lincoln in his Gettysburg Address, America was listening.

This wasn't to say her campaign was without its critics. "People are saying, 'How dare you mount a challenge to someone who's so established?'" she admitted.[131] Joe Crowley had been in elected office for thirty years and hadn't had a primary challenger since 2004. Many people were shocked she would dare to challenge someone so deeply entrenched in the Democratic party, especially given that she aligned more with the Bernie Sanders wing of the party, which was much more left-wing and progressive, than with the Hillary Clinton and Barack Obama wing, which was more moderate.

The campaign itself was an uphill battle. Crowley had way more money to fund his campaign, having raised almost $2.8 million by March 2018. AOC, on the other hand, had

129 Alexandria Ocasio-Cortez, "Hey Reddit!" Reddit, 2017.

130 "See moment Ocasio-Cortez realized victory," CNN Politics, video, 1:28.

131 "Knock Down The House | Official Trailer | Netflix," April 22, 2019, Netflix, video, 2:30.

raised only about $127,000 by that point.[132] In fact, he ended up spending eighteen times more on his campaign than she did. Crowley, as the incumbent, had more resources than Ocasio-Cortez and used those to fund more campaign ads and a proper campaign headquarters.

Compared to Crowley, things looked a little bleak for Ocasio-Cortez. "For 80 percent of this campaign, I operated out of a paper grocery bag hidden behind that bar," she said of the taqueria where she worked at the time.[133] She was constantly referred to as "Crowley's challenger" instead of "candidate for New York's fourteenth House District," and most people assumed she would lose the primary.

But she continued on with the campaign anyway. She went door-to-door, canvassing and speaking to voters like most other candidates. But what she did differently than Crowley and the Democratic "machine" was use technology and social media. She focused on getting endorsements from HuffPost, Refinery29, and other online liberal media outlets. Her advertising, in fact, was almost entirely digital, which was a departure from normal campaign methods. She also had a large Twitter following—much larger than Crowley's—and had lots of enthusiastic tweets from her supporters.[134]

The main key to AOC's success was the way she communicated on social media. Unlike many other politicians,

---

132 "Alexandria Ocasio-Cortez," Ballotpedia, Accessed June 1, 2020.

133 Hilary Cadigan, "Alexandria Ocasio-Cortez Learned Her Most Important Lessons from Restaurants," bon appétit, November 7, 2018.

134 Grace Segers, "How Alexandria Ocasio-Cortez won the race that shocked the country," City & State New York, June 27, 2018.

Ocasio-Cortez comes from a generation that grew up on social media, so she gets it. She speaks authentically rather than just spewing out her political platform like most other politicians. She uses short, punchy sentences with emojis, and her posts are emotional. She also clearly does most of her social media posting herself instead of hiring a staffer to do it, which is rare.

Crowley, on the other hand, came across as very establishment, with posts devoid of emotion or authenticity. As one article puts it, "The voters can feel Alexandria; at most, they can intellectualize Crowley."[135]

AOC consistently asked for participation and feedback from voters, rather than just donations, like most people. Her social media presence was focused on the people in her district, not herself. Crowley's social media focused on himself and the things he has done. Social media really was the cornerstone of her campaign, and it is what gave her the momentum she needed.

June 26, 2018, the day of the primary, arrived and with it, the tallying of the votes. On that night, Alexandria Ocasio-Cortez stood with her supporters in a bar in New York City, waiting for the results, waiting to find out if she would deliver a huge upset, waiting to find out if all her work would come to fruition. The bar itself was nothing special. It was dark and crowded, filled with people wearing her campaign shirts. Everyone was waiting around for news, any news.

---

135  Peter Friedman, "The 2018 Social Media Political Wars: How Ocasio-Cortez Used Social Media to Beat Joe Crowley," LiveWorld, July 6, 2018.

The votes were tallied, and the news rolled in: She did it. She won. AOC's immediate reaction was shock. Her hands covered her mouth, and all she could say was, "Oh my god!" A reporter pulled her over for an interview, saying of Ocasio-Cortez, "She's seeing herself on television right now."[136] The whole room exploded with excitement.

This, for her, was what politics is about. The people have spoken, and they have asked for change.

"This victory belongs to every single grassroots organizer, every working parent, every mom, every member of the LGBTQ community, every single person is responsible for this," she said to the reporter on Election Night.[137] This grassroots campaign, run by and for the everyday people, had overtaken the political machine. Alexandria Ocasio-Cortez didn't grow up wealthy or powerful, but she got involved in her community and made a difference. She appealed to younger voters, minority voters, and progressive voters by utilizing social media and technology and she continues to create change for her community every single day as a member of Congress. Because of her use of technology, she was able to overtake the incumbent Crowley, and she continues to use Twitter to connect with constituents and make her voice heard.

---

136  CNN Politics, "Ocasio-Cortez."

137  Ibid.

## SOCIAL MEDIA HELPS SPREAD MESSAGES

Social media has opened a lot of doors for us because it has allowed us to spread messages more quickly and to a wider range of people. It has become invaluable to us because it has given ordinary people the chance to make their voices heard and their thoughts and views known.

Emma Gonzalez, the gun control activist famous for her "We call BS" speech, is a great example of this phenomenon.

Emma's words may seem powerful on paper, but they are even more powerful when you hear her say them. It seems as though a lot of Americans agreed with that sentiment because the video of this speech went viral, and almost immediately she became a nationally known figure. Her name started trending on Twitter, and she quickly gained over a million followers.[138]

What's really amazing about Emma is she didn't even know how to use Twitter when her name started trending. She had to quickly learn from her classmates.[139] But she was able to capitalize on this sudden Twitter fame to encourage change. She and other students from Parkland continued to advocate for stricter gun control, attending town halls and giving speeches. Emma was interviewed by 60 Minutes and was on the cover of Time Magazine.

---

138  Valerie Strauss, "This Parkland student quickly amassed more Twitter followers than the NRA. Here's what she's been writing," *The Washington Post*, March 1, 2018.

139  Jonah Engel Bromwich, "How the Parkland Students Got So Good at Social Media," *The New York Times*, March 7, 2018.

Shortly after the shooting, she helped found a student-led political action committee called Never Again MSD, which advocates for stricter gun regulations. The group has a lot of support on Twitter, where it is identified by the hashtags #NeverAgain and #EnoughIsEnough. As part of this group, she helped organize the March for Our Lives in March 2018, which took place in Washington, DC, but had affiliated events all over the country. The DC march had over two hundred thousand people in attendance, and if the other marches across the US are included, the estimated participation was around 1.2 million people.[140, 141]

The goal of the march was to convince legislators to pass legislation that would prevent gun violence, including measures such as closing the gun show loophole, requiring universal background checks, and banning assault weapons. Emma gave a speech at the March for Our Lives, and that speech, she noted, was the same length as the shooting at her high school—six minutes and twenty seconds. "Everyone, absolutely everyone in the Douglas community was altered," she said. After stating the names of the seventeen people lost that day, she remained silent for the rest of the six minutes and twenty seconds. She ended with a call to action. "Fight for your lives before it's someone else's job."[142] By the end of her speech, many people in the crowd were crying. In fact, Emma herself had to keep wiping away tears. This was not

140  "How many people attended March for Our Lives? Crowd in DC estimated at 200,000," CBS News, March 25, 2018.

141  German Lopez, "It's official: March for Our Lives was one of the biggest youth protests since the Vietnam War," *Vox*, March 26, 2018.

142  "Emma Gonzalez March for Our Lives Speech Transcript," Rev, March 24, 2018.

an easy job she was doing, and it took a lot of strength for her to get up and give the speech.

Because of Emma's activism—and the activism of other survivors of this shooting—the Florida legislature passed a law called the Marjory Stoneman Douglas High School Public Safety Act. This law, passed in March 2018, raised the minimum legal age to purchase a firearm in Florida from eighteen to twenty-one and established waiting periods, mandatory background checks, and certain restrictions on who is able to purchase a firearm.[143] This law was the direct result of Emma and her friends' persistence in fighting for stricter gun control.

They have also succeeded in registering more young people to vote. In the summer and fall of 2018, Never Again MSD, the group that organized the March for Our Lives, registered over fifty thousand new voters on its "Road to Change" tour. They traveled around the country, focusing primarily on those who just turned eighteen or who would be by the November election.

Emma is now twenty years old and her activism has not stopped. She graduated from high school in 2018, just a few months after the shooting, and now attends the New College of Florida. She remains active on social media, where she still pushes for gun control reforms and gets young people registered to vote. Emma is quite remarkable because she was able to stand up after a tragedy and use her newly found

---

143 "Florida Senate passes Marjory Stoneman Douglas High School Public Safety Act," Florida Trend, March 6, 2018.

voice to push for ways to avoid this type of tragedy in the future. Though the federal government has not passed any comprehensive gun control legislation, Emma succeeded in getting more young people to vote and in getting gun control legislation passed in Florida. Both of these accomplishments have had a substantial impact on her community, and she has inspired young people all across the country to get involved in their democracy.

Emma's story shows us just how powerful social media can be. Because of the hashtags used by Never Again MSD, the issue of gun violence became an issue of national importance, and it has not gone away. The 1.2 million people who participated in anti-gun violence marches would not have been inspired to do so if not for Emma's viral speech and her use of social media. This shows us that social media—and Twitter especially—can be extremely effective in spreading messages and in creating real change in our communities.

## SOCIAL MEDIA PROVIDES A VOICE TO ALL PEOPLE

When I was a freshman in college, I was a writer for the Odyssey Online, a publication that allows people to publish articles on a wide range of topics. It was through this platform that I really found my voice; I wrote several different articles about politics and I always shared them to Facebook so people could see them. Writing about politics in this setting gave me a place in which I could insert my voice and make it heard by the general public.

One article in particular really sticks out to me when I think of all the articles I wrote. It was about the 2017 Women's March on Washington, entitled, "Why I Marched." When I shared it publicly to Facebook after it was published on the site, the article started being read by many people, way more than any of my other articles. I really felt like that article had given me the chance to express my viewpoint on the current state of politics and some of the frustrations I was feeling. Posting it to social media so more people could see it made me feel even more heard. In short, social media gave me a voice when I didn't feel like I had one, which was so important to me.

I am, of course, not the only person who has gained a voice through social media. Camryn Cobb is a consumer journalism major at the University of Georgia who didn't start getting involved in politics until she started college. During her freshman year, after going to a Young Democrats meeting and hearing the county commissioner speak, she got involved in a gentrification project they were working on. This project got her really interested in local politics.

Camryn also joined a club called Dawgs 4 Abrams, which strategized different ways to garner support for Stacey Abrams. Abrams was the Democratic candidate for governor in Georgia in 2018, running against Republican Brian Kemp. Abrams was the first African American woman to be the nominee for governor of a major party, and this was really important to Camryn. "I truly felt like, due to the fact that she was a minority and a woman, she would have to fight ten times harder to win, and I was dedicated to helping her."

The way Camryn tried to help Abrams was by encouraging people to vote. She did this by utilizing social media. "The way I got my friends to vote is literally Snapchat! I swear I posted a Snapchat about this election nearly every day." She convinced many of her friends to register to vote or to check their registration status by providing links on her Snapchat story to do so.

"It was super important for me to utilize my platform in ways that would be beneficial and fight to provide proper representation for people in my state," she said. Although Stacey Abrams lost the gubernatorial election, Camryn managed to have a positive impact in her community, as she convinced people to vote who otherwise would not have. "Many people told me they only registered and voted because of me."

Camryn's story shows that social media can be a powerful tool for change. She managed to convince more people to vote, and more people voting is always a good thing. Regardless of the outcome of the election, higher voter turnout means more people's voices are being heard, and Camryn managed to make that happen by using social media. In a pre-social media world, this kind of change would not be possible, so social media has been a huge advancement in our society. Camryn's use of this tool is simple and effective, and it gives her a voice. Using social media is a very easy way to get involved and make a difference.

As we can see from the stories in this chapter, social media can be a very effective way to both make your opinions heard and stay up-to-date on what is happening. Currently, 79 percent of Americans have some form of social media, which means most of us already have the tools to find our voice and to make a difference.[144] More people should be using these platforms to become activists and create change because it takes very little effort and can have a very positive effect on the political landscape.

144 J. Clement, "Share of US population who use social media 2008–2019," Statista, May 19, 2020.

# APPENDIX

———

**INTRODUCTION**

Manning, Jennifer. *Membership of the 116th Congress: A Profile.* Report prepared for Members and Committees of Congress. Washington, D.C.: Congressional Research Service, 2020. Accessed April 22, 2020. *https://fas.org/sgp/crs/misc/R45583.pdf.*

Rutgers University Center for Youth Political Participation. "The Virginia State Legislature." Updated November 18, 2019. *http://cypp.rutgers.edu/yelp/current-data/the-virginia-state-legislature/#a3.*


**CHAPTER 1**

Alchin, Linda. "Franklin Roosevelt Presidential Cabinet." US Presidents. January 2016. Accessed April 24, 2020. *http://www.presidential-power.org/presidential-cabinets/presidential-cabinet-franklin-roosevelt.htm.*

Americans Who Tell the Truth. "Barbara Johns." Accessed May 26, 2020. *https://www.americanswhotellthetruth.org/portraits/barbara-johns.*

Atlanta Journal-Constitution. "Diane Nash." February 1, 2017. *https://www.ajc.com/news/national/diane-nash/7bAodNsSPqT-DcEOVCkvgdK/*.

Avila, Theresa. "18 Quotes About Political Action That Will Fire You Up to Vote." Girlboss, November 2, 2018. *https://www.girlboss.com/identity/political-quotes-women*.

Baynes, Leonard M. "The Celebration of the 40th Anniversary of Ronald H. Brown's Graduation from St. John's School of Law." *Journal of Civil Rights and Economic Development* 25, no. 1 (Fall 2010): 1-45. *https://scholarship.law.stjohns.edu/cgi/viewcontent.cgi?article=1645&context=jcred*.

Billington, Monroe. "Susanna Madora Salter First Woman Mayor." *Kansas Historical Quarterly* 21, no. 3 (Autumn 1954): 173-183. *https://www.kshs.org/p/kansas-historical-quarterly-susanna-madora-salter/13106*.

Breitman, Jessica. "Frances Perkins." FDR Library & Museum. Accessed April 24, 2020. *https://www.fdrlibrary.org/perkins*.

Clinton Presidential Library. "Hillary R. Clinton Biography." Accessed May 26, 2020. *https://www.clintonlibrary.gov/clintons/hillary-r-clinton-biography/*.

CNN Politics. "Hillary Clinton's DNC speech: full text." Updated July 29, 2016. *https://www.cnn.com/2016/07/28/politics/hillary-clinton-speech-prepared-remarks-transcript/index.html*.

Eriksmoen, Curt. "History: ND elected first woman to be administrator of a state office."*Bismarck Tribune*, April 25, 2010. *https://bismarcktribune.com/news/columnists/curt-eriksmoen/history-nd-elected-first-woman-to-be-administrator-of-a/article_6a517d7e-4eff-11df-8b8c-001cc4c002e0.html*.

Hayward, Nancy. "Susan B. Anthony." National Women's History Museum. 2018. *https://www.womenshistory.org/education-resources/biographies/susan-b-anthony.*

The King Center. "Mrs. Coretta Scott King." About Mrs. King. Accessed April 24, 2020. *https://thekingcenter.org/about-mrs-king/.*

Levitz, Eric. "Trump Has Turned Millions of Americans Into Activists." *Intelligencer,* April 6, 2018. *https://nymag.com/intelligencer/2018/04/trump-has-turned-millions-of-americans-into-activists.html.*

Lowen, Linda. "Meet the Female Supreme Court Justices." ThoughtCo. Updated October 2, 2019. *https://www.thoughtco.com/history-of-women-on-the-supreme-court-3533864.*

MacLean, Maggie. "Victoria Woodhull." The Ohio State University Department of History. Accessed April 24, 2020. *https://ehistory.osu.edu/biographies/victoria-woodhull.*

Manning, Jennifer. *Membership of the 116th Congress: A Profile.* Report prepared for Members and Committees of Congress. Washington, D.C.: Congressional Research Service, 2020. Accessed April 22, 2020. *https://fas.org/sgp/crs/misc/R45583.pdf.*

Michals, Debra. "Elizabeth Cady Stanton." National Women's History Museum. 2017. *https://www.womenshistory.org/education-resources/biographies/elizabeth-cady-stanton.*

Michals, Debra. "Gloria Steinem." National Women's History Museum. 2017. *https://www.womenshistory.org/education-resources/biographies/gloria-steinem.*

National Archives. "Jeannette Rankin: The woman who voted to give women the right to vote." Pieces of History. January 26, 2017. *https://prologue.blogs.archives.gov/2017/01/26/jeannette-*

*rankin-the-woman-who-voted-to-give-women-the-right-to-vote/.*

National Women's History Museum. "Anna Dickinson." Accessed May 26, 2020. *https://web.archive.org/web/20161108020740/ https://www.nwhm.org/education-resources/biography/biographies/anna-dickinson/.*

Rea, Tom. "The Ambition of Nellie Tayloe Ross." *WyoHistory.org*, November 8, 2014. *https://www.wyohistory.org/encyclopedia/ ambition-nellie-tayloe-ross.*

Rutgers University. "Milestones for Women in American Politics." Center for American Women and Politics. Accessed April 24, 2020. *https://cawp.rutgers.edu/facts/milestones-for-women.*

Rutgers University. "History of Women Governors." Center for American Women and Politics. Accessed April 24, 2020. *https:// cawp.rutgers.edu/history-women-governors.*

Rutgers University. "Women Appointed to Presidential Cabinets." Center for American Women and Politics. April 12, 2019. *http:// www.cawp.rutgers.edu/sites/default/files/resources/womenappt-dtoprescabinets.pdf.*

"Sisters who participated in 1963 Children's March to speak at Smithfield Library today." *AL.com,* March 10, 2016. *https://www. al.com/press-releases/2016/03/sisters_who_participated_in_19. html.*

SNCC Digital Gateway. "Diane Nash." Accessed April 24, 2020. *https://snccdigital.org/people/diane-nash-bevel/.*

Stolberg, Sheryl Gay. "Nancy Pelosi, Icon of Female Power, Will Reclaim Role as Speaker and Seal a Place in History." *The New York Times,* January 2, 2019. *https://www.nytimes. com/2019/01/02/us/politics/nancy-pelosi-house-speaker.html.*

United States House of Representatives. "Rankin, Jeannette." History, Art & Archives. Accessed April 24, 2020. *https://history.house.gov/People/Listing/R/RANKIN,-Jeannette-(R000055)/.*

We've Got a Job. "Audrey Faye Hendricks." Major Players. Accessed May 26, 2020. *http://www.wevegotajob.com/major-players-audrey.html.*

**CHAPTER 2**

Avila, Theresa. "18 Quotes About Political Action That Will Fire You Up to Vote." Girlboss, November 2, 2018. *https://www.girlboss.com/identity/political-quotes-women.*

Crockett, Emily. "Hillary Clinton: 'I had to learn as a young woman to control my emotions.'" *Vox,* September 8, 2016. *https://www.vox.com/2016/9/8/12851878/hillary-clinton-control-emotions-sexism-humans-new-york.*

Cummings, William. "Louisiana police officer's Facebook post says Alexandria Ocasio-Cortez 'needs a round,' report says." *USA Today,* Updated July 23, 2019. *https://www.usatoday.com/story/news/politics/2019/07/22/alexandria-ocasio-cortez-threatened-police-officer/1793131001/.*

Hayes, Christal. "Trump supporter threatens to kill Democratic lawmakers over Rep. Omar's 9/11 comments, docs say." *USA Today,* Updated April 19, 2019. *https://www.usatoday.com/story/news/politics/2019/04/19/rep-ilhan-omar-rashida-tlaib-targeted-racist-death-threats-man-arrested/3522754002/.*

Horowitz, Juliana Menasce, Ruth Igielnik, and Kim Parker. "Women and Leadership 2018." Pew Research Center. September 20, 2018. *https://www.pewsocialtrends.org/2018/09/20/women-and-leadership-2018/.*

International Knowledge Network of Women in Politics. "Violence Against Women in Politics." Accessed April 24, 2020. *https://www.iknowpolitics.org/en/discuss/e-discussions/violence-against-women-politics-0.*

Mathiesen, Vicki. "Clinton shows 'no emotion, no heart no soul.'" Letter to the editor, *Fresno Bee*, 2016. *https://www.fresnobee.com/opinion/letters-to-the-editor/article106227012.html.*

Milligan, Susan. "Women Candidates Still Tagged as Too 'Emotional' to Hold Office." *US News & World Report*, April 16, 2019. *https://www.usnews.com/news/politics/articles/2019-04-16/women-candidates-still-tagged-as-too-emotional-to-hold-office.*

Murray, Jeff, and Christal Hayes. "'I'll put a bullet in her': Trump supporter charged with threatening to kill Rep. Ilhan Omar." *USA Today*, Updated April 7, 2019. *https://www.usatoday.com/story/news/politics/2019/04/05/ilhan-omar-death-threat-leads-to-arrest-of-new-york-man/3379387002/.*

Ross, Janell. "Donald Trump thinks Hillary Clinton, a lady running for president, is crazy." *The Washington Post*, August 8, 2016. *https://www.washingtonpost.com/news/the-fix/wp/2016/08/08/donald-trump-thinks-hillary-clinton-a-lady-running-for-president-is-crazy/.*

UN Women. "Violence Against Women in Politics." 2014. *https://www.unwomen.org/en/digital-library/publications/2014/6/violence-against-women-in-politics.*

Vezner, Tad. "Death threat allegedly called in to office of MN lawmaker who sponsored gun-control bill." *Twin Cities Pioneer Press*, March 6, 2018. *https://www.twincities.com/2018/03/06/death-threat-allegedly-called-in-to-office-mn-lawmaker-who-sponsored-gun-control-bill/.*

**CHAPTER 3**

Albright, Madeleine. "A hidden reality: Violence against women in politics." *CNN*, March 8, 2016. *https://www.cnn.com/2016/03/07/opinions/madelaine-albright-protect-women-in-politics/index.html.*

Avila, Theresa. "18 Quotes About Political Action That Will Fire You Up to Vote." Girlboss, November 2, 2018. *https://www.girlboss.com/identity/political-quotes-women.*

Deckman, Melissa. "What Women Want: Issue Priorities for Women Voters in Election 2018." Gender Watch 2018. August 10, 2018. *http://www.genderwatch2018.org/what-women-want/.*

Fingerhut, Hannah. "Support steady for same-sex marriage and acceptance of homosexuality." Pew Research Center. May 12, 2016. *https://www.pewresearch.org/fact-tank/2016/05/12/support-steady-for-same-sex-marriage-and-acceptance-of-homosexuality/.*

Gambino, Lauren. "'Try to keep up': how Ocasio-Cortez upended politics in her first year in office." *The Guardian*, December 24, 2019. *https://www.theguardian.com/us-news/2019/dec/24/alexandria-ocasio-cortez-aoc-first-year-congress.*

Hamilton College. "Political Attitudes of Young Americans." Accessed May 26, 2020. *https://www.hamilton.edu/news/polls/political-attitudes-of-young-americans.*

Kellman, Laurie and Hannah Fingerhut. "Young people are looking for younger leaders, poll finds." *PBS News Hour*, July 30, 2018. *https://www.pbs.org/newshour/politics/young-people-are-looking-for-younger-leaders-poll-finds.*

Kliff, Sarah. "The research is clear: electing more women changes how government works." *Vox,* March 8, 2017. *https://www.vox.*

*com/2016/7/27/12266378/electing-women-congress-hillary-clinton.*

Knoema. "US Population by Age and Generation in 2020." Updated April 16, 2020. *https://knoema.com/egyydzc/us-population-by-age-and-generation-in-2020.*

Morrison, Dan and Chris Tyree. "Generation Activist." Orb. Accessed May 26, 2020. *https://orbmedia.org/stories/generation-activist/multimedia.*

Pepera, Sandra. "Why Women in Politics?" Women Deliver, February 28, 2018. *https://womendeliver.org/2018/why-women-in-politics/.*

Richards, Cecile. "The political progress women have made—and what's next." Filmed November 2018 at TEDWomen 2018. Video, 16:56. *https://www.ted.com/talks/cecile_richards_the_political_progress_women_have_made_and_what_s_next/up-next?language=en.*

Rutgers University Center for Youth Political Participation. "The 116th United States Congress." Updated April 18, 2019. *http://cypp.rutgers.edu/yelp/current-data/116th-congress/.*

**CHAPTER 4**

Count Love. "Statistics." Updated May 26, 2020. *https://countlove.org/statistics.html.*

K, Lidiya. "How 15 Successful People Describe Passion." Let's Reach Success. January 24, 2020. *https://letsreachsuccess.com/describe-passion/.*

Kerpen, Dave. "15 Inspiring Quotes on Passion (Get Back to What You Love)." Inc.com. March 27, 2014. *https://www.inc.com/dave-kerpen/15-quotes-on-passion-to-inspire-a-better-life.html.*

Levitz, Eric. "Trump Has Turned Millions of Americans Into Activists." *Intelligencer,* April 6, 2018. *https://nymag.com/intelligencer/2018/04/trump-has-turned-millions-of-americans-into-activists.html.*

Mohamed, Besheer. "New estimates show U.S. Muslim population continues to grow." Pew Research Center. January 3, 2018. *https://www.pewresearch.org/fact-tank/2018/01/03/new-estimates-show-u-s-muslim-population-continues-to-grow/.*

Raab, Diana. "What's Your Passion?" Psychology Today. June 12, 2017. *https://www.psychologytoday.com/us/blog/the-empowerment-diary/201706/whats-your-passion.*

Raphelson, Samantha. "Muslim Americans Running For Office In Highest Numbers Since 2001." *NPR,* July 18, 2018. *https://www.npr.org/2018/07/18/630132952/muslim-americans-running-for-office-in-highest-numbers-since-2001.*

Virginia Public Access Project. "General Assembly Turnout Varied in 2015." August 26, 2019. *https://www.vpap.org/visuals/visual/general-assembly-voter-turnout-2015/.*

YPulse. "The 15 Issues Gen Z & Millennials Are Most Passionate About." February 26, 2018. *https://www.ypulse.com/article/2018/02/26/15-issues-gen-z-millennials-are-most-passionate-about/.*

## CHAPTER 5

Fletcher, Adam. "Quotes about Youth + Social Change." Freechild Institute. January 28, 2020. *https://freechild.org/quotes-about-youth-changing-the-world/*.

Merelli, Annalisa. "Trump is trying to make it too expensive for poor American immigrants to stay." *Quartz*, December 6, 2019. *https://qz.com/1759717/uscis-may-raise-the-cost-of-us-citizenship-applications-by-61-percent/*.

Orofino, Alessandra. "It's our city. Let's fix it." Filmed October 2014 at TEDGlobal 2014. Video, 15:08. *https://www.ted.com/talks/alessandra_orofino_it_s_our_city_let_s_fix_it*.

Vandermaas-Peeler, Alex, Daniel Cox, Maxine Najle, Molly Fisch-Friedman, and Rob Griffin. "American Democracy in Crisis: Civic Engagement, Young Adult Activism, and the 2018 Midterm Elections." Public Religion Research Institute. October 11, 2018. *https://www.prri.org/research/american-democracy-in-crisis-civic-engagement-young-adult-activism-and-the-2018-midterm-elections/*.

Weiner, Rachel. "Outside groups launch attacks in Va. congressional race." *The Washington Post*, October 14, 2014. *https://www.washingtonpost.com/local/virginia-politics/outside-groups-launch-attacks-in-va-congressional-race/2014/10/14/ae3be3be-53c1-11e4-ba4b-f6333e2c0453_story.html*.

## CHAPTER 6

Bowerman, Mary. "Watch: 6-year-old Sophie Cruz captures hearts at massive Women's March." *USA Today*, January 21, 2017. *https://www.usatoday.com/story/news/politics/onpoli-*

tics/2017/01/21/watch-6-year-old-sophie-cruz-capture-hearts-massive-womens-march/96889558/.

Bradham, Bre. "Q&A: Young politicians explain what it's like being college-aged elected officials." *The Chronicle*, March 6, 2019. *https://www.dukechronicle.com/article/2019/03/garrett-cole-cassandra-levesque-college-age-elected-officials-qa.*

Copeny, Mari's official website. "About Mari." Accessed May 29, 2020. *https://www.maricopeny.com/about.*

CNN. ""Florida student Emma Gonzalez to lawmakers and gun advocates: 'We call BS.'" Updated February 17, 2018. *https://www.cnn.com/2018/02/17/us/florida-student-emma-gonzalez-speech/index.html.*

Danielli. "Meet 8-Year-Old Latina Immigration Activist Sophie Cruz Who Is Changing The Conversation On Immigrant Rights." *mitú*, March 21, 2019. *https://wearemitu.com/things-that-matter/politics/latina-immigration-activist-sophie-cruz/.*

Denchak, Melissa. "Flint Water Crisis: Everything You Need to Know." Natural Resources Defense Council. November 8, 2018. *https://www.nrdc.org/stories/flint-water-crisis-everything-you-need-know.*

Fletcher, Adam. "Quotes about Youth + Social Change." Freechild Institute. January 28, 2020. *https://freechild.org/quotes-about-youth-changing-the-world/.*

"Future Women of America: Meet Mari Copeny." November 30, 2018. Brit + Co. Video, 3:08. *https://www.youtube.com/watch?v=ML2dRP9i3FQ.*

Germano, Beth. "19-Year-Old Ready To Become Youngest New Hampshire Lawmaker." CBS Boston, November 27, 2018. *https://*

boston.cbslocal.com/2018/11/27/cassandra-levesque-new-hamp-shire-state-house-legislature/.

Giffords Law Center. "Florida Gun Laws." Accessed May 29, 2020. https://lawcenter.giffords.org/gun-laws/state-law/florida/.

"Mari Copeny WINS Best in Activism || Shorty Awards 2019." May 6, 2019. Shorty Awards. Video, 2:50. https://www.youtube.com/watch?v=IhJmKy4_nmE.

National Conference of State Legislatures. "Women in State Legislatures for 2019." Women's Legislative Network. July 25, 2019. https://www.ncsl.org/legislators-staff/legislators/womens-legislative-network/women-in-state-legislatures-for-2019.aspx.

"New Hampshire State Rep. Cassie Levesque Wants To End Child Marriage." NowThis. Produced by Jackie Padilla. Video, 2:42.

Robinson, Melia and Skye Gould. "There were 340 mass shootings in the US in 2018—here's the full list." Business Insider, December 31, 2018. https://www.businessinsider.com/how-many-mass-shootings-in-america-this-year-2018-2.

San Jose Museum of Art. "A Mural of Hope." Accessed June 25, 2020. https://sjmusart.org/mural-hope.

Selby, Daniele. "Child Marriage is Legal in the US. How You Can Help End it." Global Citizen. September 3, 2019. https://www.globalcitizen.org/en/content/child-marriage-in-the-us-what-to-know/.

Silverstein, Jason. "There were more mass shootings than days in 2019." CBS News, January 2, 2020. https://www.cbsnews.com/news/mass-shootings-2019-more-than-days-365/.

Taylor, Derrick Bryson. "Trump Mocks Greta Thunberg on Twitter, and She Jabs Back." The New York Times, December 12, 2019.

*https://www.nytimes.com/2019/12/12/us/politics/greta-thun-berg-trump.html.*

Taylor, Kate. "In New Class of Young Lawmakers, a Former Girl Scout Goes to the Statehouse." *The New York Times,* November 13, 2018. *https://www.nytimes.com/2018/11/13/us/young-candi-dates-elections.html.*

Thunberg, Greta. "The disarming case to act right now on climate change." Filmed November 2018 at TEDxStockholm. Video, 11:04. *https://www.ted.com/talks/greta_thunberg_the_disarm-ing_case_to_act_right_now_on_climate_change.*

United Nations Framework Convention on Climate Change. "The Paris Agreement." Process and meetings. Accessed May 29, 2020. *https://unfccc.int/process-and-meetings/the-paris-agree-ment/the-paris-agreement.*

Willingham, Leah. "Now a legislator, Girl Scout returns to State House to raise marriage age to 18." *Concord Monitor,* February 19, 2019. *https://www.concordmonitor.com/Cassie-Levesque-re-turns-with-another-child-marriage-bill-23591132.*

## CHAPTER 7

Anderson, Kare. "Be an opportunity maker." Filmed September 2014 at TED@IBM. Video, 9:38. *https://www.ted.com/talks/kare_anderson_be_an_opportunity_maker.*

Currence, Melissa and Amy Hjerstedt. "Episode 18: Young Leader in Her Own Words." July 7, 2018. In *What Would Alice Paul Do?* Podcast, 25:14. *https://www.alicepaulpodcast.com/pod-cast/2018/7/7/episode-18-lessons-learned-from-an-emerging-civic-leader.*

SUCCESS Staff. "13 Quotes to Motivate You to Seize Opportunities." SUCCESS. May 2, 2019. *https://www.success.com/13-opportunity-quotes/.*

Virginia Public Access Project. "House of Delegates District 87." Accessed June 1, 2020. *https://www.vpap.org/offices/house-of-delegates-87/district/.*

## CHAPTER 8

Ballotpedia. "Alexandria Ocasio-Cortez." Accessed June 1, 2020. *https://ballotpedia.org/Alexandria_Ocasio-Cortez.*

Bromwich, Jonah Engel. "How the Parkland Students Got So Good at Social Media." *The New York Times,* March 7, 2018. *https://www.nytimes.com/2018/03/07/us/parkland-students-social-media.html.*

Cadigan, Hilary. "Alexandria Ocasio-Cortez Learned Her Most Important Lessons from Restaurants." bon appétit. November 7, 2018. *https://www.bonappetit.com/story/alexandria-ocasio-cortez-lessons-from-restaurants.*

CBS News. "How many people attended March for Our Lives? Crowd in D.C. estimated at 200,000." March 25, 2018. *https://www.cbsnews.com/news/march-for-our-lives-crowd-size-estimated-200000-people-attended-d-c-march/.*

Clement, J. "Share of U.S. population who use social media 2008-2019." Statista. May 19, 2020. *https://www.statista.com/statistics/273476/percentage-of-us-population-with-a-social-network-profile/.*

Florida Trend. "Florida Senate passes Marjory Stoneman Douglas High School Public Safety Act." March 6, 2018. *https://www.floridatrend.com/article/24092/florida-senate-passes-marjory-stoneman-douglas-high-school-public-safety-act.*

Friedman, Peter. "The 2018 Social Media Political Wars: How Oca-sio-Cortez Used Social Media to Beat Joe Crowley." LiveWorld. July 6, 2018. *https://www.liveworld.com/2018-social-media-po-litical-wars-how-ocasio-cortez-used-social-media-beat-joe-crowley/.*

"Knock Down The House | Official Trailer | Netflix." April 22, 2019. Netflix. Video, 2:30. *https://www.youtube.com/watch?time_con-tinue=50&v=_wGZc8ZjFY4&feature=emb_logo.*

Lopez, German. "It's official: March for Our Lives was one of the biggest youth protests since the Vietnam War." *Vox,* March 26, 2018. *https://www.vox.com/policy-and-poli-tics/2018/3/26/17160646/march-for-our-lives-crowd-size-count.*

Manskar, Noah. "What is 'Blackout Tuesday'? Trend floods social media amid George Floyd protests." *New York Post,* June 2, 2020. *https://nypost.com/2020/06/02/what-is-blackout-tuesday-everything-to-know-about-the-movement/.*

"Mari Copeny WINS Best in Activism || Shorty Awards 2019." May 6, 2019. Shorty Awards. Video, 2:50. *https://www.youtube.com/watch?v=IhJmKy4_nmE.*

Ocasio-Cortez, Alexandria. "Hey Reddit!" Reddit, 2017. *https://www.reddit.com/r/SandersForPresident/comments/6ftvhu/hey_reddit_i_am_alexandria_ocasiocortez_us/.*

Pencak, Silvia. "Top 50+ Social Media Quotes." Powerful Life Consulting. Accessed June 1, 2020. *https://silviapencak.com/top-50-social-media-quotes/.*

Rev. "Emma Gonzalez March for Our Lives Speech Transcript." March 24, 2018. *https://www.rev.com/blog/transcripts/emma-gonzalez-march-for-our-lives-speech-transcript.*

"See moment Ocasio-Cortez realized victory." CNN Politics. Video, 1:28. *https://www.cnn.com/videos/politics/2018/06/27/alexandria-ocasio-cortez-new-york-reaction-vpx.ny1.*

Segers, Grace. "How Alexandria Ocasio-Cortez won the race that shocked the country." City & State New York. June 27, 2018. *https://www.cityandstateny.com/articles/politics/campaigns-elections/how-alexandria-ocasio-cortez-won-race-shocked-country.html.*

Shirky, Clay. "How social media can make history." Filmed June 2009 at TED@State. Video, 15:33. *https://www.ted.com/talks/clay_shirky_how_social_media_can_make_history.*

Strauss, Valerie. "This Parkland student quickly amassed more Twitter followers than the NRA. Here's what she's been writing." *The Washington Post,* March 1, 2018. *https://www.washingtonpost.com/news/answer-sheet/wp/2018/03/01/this-parkland-student-quickly-amassed-more-twitter-followers-than-the-nra-heres-what-shes-been-writing/.*

"The Courage to Change | Alexandria Ocasio-Cortez." May 30, 2018. Alexandria Ocasio-Cortez. Video, 2:08. *https://www.youtube.com/watch?reload=9&v=rq3QXIVRobs.*

# ACKNOWLEDGMENTS

———

When I first set out to write this book, I never realized how much work it would take and how many steps there were to get it written and published. I have been lucky enough to have a whole network of people willing and able to support every step of this journey. It has long been a dream of mine to write a book, and achieving this dream would not have been possible without my support system.

Thank you, first and foremost, to my parents. You have encouraged me and motivated me, and you have been a supporter of my writing from the very beginning. This book could not have happened without your constant support, and I owe it all to you.

Thank you to all the friends and family who witnessed the many, many hours I spent writing and who supported me emotionally as the first draft manuscript deadline got closer and closer. Thank you to everyone who ever called me an author and for helping me believe I am one. Thank you especially to Julian, whose unwavering support motivated me to keep writing.

Thank you to Eric Koester, Brian Bies, and the staff at New Degree Press for giving me the tools to write and publish this book. A special thank you to my editors, Cassandra Caswell and Natalie Bailey, for pushing me in the right direction and for reading my writing even in its very early stages.

And finally, thank you to everyone who: gave me their time for a personal interview; pre-ordered the e-book, paperback, or multiple copies to make publishing possible; participated in my Instagram fundraiser bingo; helped spread the word about *The Marching Women*; and helped me publish a book I am proud of. I am sincerely grateful for all of your help and I could not have done this without you.

Lauren Ahart
Stephen and Wendy Ahart
Hilary Barnes
Jessica Bernier
Harsha Bilwani
Olivia Bissell
Jackson Blodgett
Ann Bride*
William Brosseau
Sarah Bruns
Lucia Butler
Vanessa Cai*
Weidong Cai
and Running Pan*
Pat and Ed Campbell
Michelle Cantrell
Kathleen Chellman
Gopi Chigurupati

Camryn Cobb~
Lisa Collins
Jill Conner
Dan Connolly
Denise Cope
Emma Crawford*
Megan Croom
Allene Curto
Owen Darcy*
Eryn Dolan*
Tristan Dunn
Allison Engel
Eileen Feigenbaum
Claudia Ferrero
Jessica Findley
Barbara Fink*
Victoria Gerardi
Caroline Gerenyi

Allison Greenday~
Lucy Greenman~
Maura Greenman
Carlina Haden
Dana Hamerschlag
Elizabeth Hayes
Julian Hayes*
Megan Herzog
Isaiah Hicks
Kathleen Hocker
Kira Hoilman
Marsha Hollar
McKenna Holman
Sara Beth Holman
Maya Hossain~
Reagan Jackson
Sarah Jedrzejczak
Tracy Johnson
Delaney Kirr
Eric Koester
Carolyn Krafft
Mary Kunkle
Anna Ledwin
Anne Lemma
Brian and Sheryl Lemma*
Wayne Lemma
Wendy Lipshultz
Stephanie Lodico
Laura Lokos
Dawn Lowe*
Devin MacGoy
Jennie MacGoy

Kimberly
and Mark Masterson
Sara Mattavelli
Terry McDougall
David Medinets
Diane Morris
Davidson Norris*
Laura Norris
Ayse Ozkan
Carolyn Pennebaker
Cameron Poland
Dana Poon
Gwyneth Pudner
Emily Ratliff
Karin Right-Nolan
Alyssa Roberts
Josie Roberts
Dena Robinson
Tom Rodgers
Savannah Rogers~
Tami Rotem
Megan Rouch
Scott Saas
Aparna Sarin
Sheila Schlimme*
Dylan Schuler
Sandy Scott
Jack Shangraw
Jo Sherwood
Mattie Sherwood
Ha Young Shin
Alyssa Slovin

Earle Smola
Brianna Starkovski
Tate Stevens
Marian Stiffler
Caitlin Stow*
Angi Strauss
Sarah Swenson
Brendan Switts*
Cassie Szumigala
Pooja Tanjore~
Kristen Tate

Nancy Tessman
Viji Thatai
Caleb Turner
Sharon Ungrady
Jennifer Warmsbecker
Gerry Watterson
Cathy Whitesell
Renata Wilson
Charlynda Winkley
Ian Wright

Key: *multiple copies/campaign contributions,
    ~featured interviewee